the analysis
of delinquent
behavior

the analysis of delinquent behavior

A STRUCTURAL APPROACH

JOHN M. MARTIN

JOSEPH P. FITZPATRICK

ROBERT E. GOULD, M.D.

 RANDOM HOUSE   NEW YORK

preface

This book, together with a companion volume, *Case Studies in the Analysis of Delinquent Behavior,* now in preparation, is meant to be used in conjunction with *Delinquent Behavior: A Redefinition of the Problem,* published in 1965. The three, published as Studies in Sociology by Random House, will report much of what has been learned during six years of involvement in the delinquency field by a professional team operating at Fordham University. During the last three years the work of the Fordham group was cosponsored by the Graduate School of Social Work at New York University. The task began in 1962 with an invitation from Lincoln Hall, a private training school in New York, to examine its program from a sociological perspective for the purpose of recommending basic changes in its approach to the delinquency problem. A second phase began in 1965 with initial efforts to develop further and then teach the theoretical orientation first proposed in *Delinquent Behavior* and the research methodology for implementing that perspective which, in a more advanced stage, is presented in the present volume and in the case book now being written. Starting in 1966, a third phase sought to apply the emerging orientation and methodology within the structure of the Family Court in New York City with a view to identifying a new environmentally oriented model for juvenile court practice. The fourth and final phase was devoted to the design of a model program for Lincoln Hall, which would enable that school, whose main campus is situated in suburban Westchester County, to become more thoroughly and intimately related to the slum communities of New York City in which most of the boys it cares for live.

Any programs directed toward implementing the orientation outlined in the three books would seem best managed and adapted by a coalition of urban-interest groups. Professors and students, such as those whose work is reported here and in the two companion volumes, will not be able to push much further the practical implications of what is being offered without the help and participation of others. Three sets of "others" can be specified: the economic and political elite who run things from the top in welfare and in every other sector of our society; the welfare professionals who manage things at the agency level and who stand in great danger of simply serving, to use Herbert Gans' term, as "caretakers" of the poor; and, as almost everybody by this time knows, the poor themselves, especially those segments of the minority group poor whose youngsters so frequently end up receiving the care of the juvenile justice system. It will not be easy to enlist the active alliance of all four interest groups—professors and students, community elite, welfare professionals, and the most disadvantaged from among the poor— in mapping an environmentally oriented strategy to bear on delinquency in its urban context. Nor will the task of building such an alliance ever be fully completed and finished. It will grow and prosper to the degree that the four community groups involved can effectively relate to one another as partners and, in the process, develop the capacity to negotiate and accommodate their many conflicting interests.

Funds for the support of the research, demonstration, and planning projects upon which this book is based were provided by the Office of Juvenile Delinquency and Youth Development, United States Department of Health, Education, and Welfare, by the Board of Managers of Lincoln Hall, and by Fordham University.

Of the many professionals who participated with us in our joint venture, Charles F. Grosser deserves particular mention. As Associate Director of the Juvenile Court Community Development Project, described in later chapters, he and Selma H. Stevens ran the New York University field work unit of that project which in 1966–1968 operated at the neighborhood level in the East Tremont section of the central Bronx in New York City. But Dr. Grosser did much more than direct the field work unit—as an articulate and tough-minded community organizer, he put himself and, hopefully, helped put the rest of us more concretely and firmly on the side of those who receive rather than dispense welfare services for the poor. It is one thing to understand the issues involved from a theoretical and intellectual level; it is quite another to make practical decisions which do not get aborted, or end in political disasters. Professor Grosser has this talent for decision-making, and he did his best to keep our joint efforts on the right course.

Much of the source material used in writing this book originally appeared as unpublished working papers prepared by researchers working under the supervision and direction of John Martin. In part, Chapter 2 on the method of situational analysis is based on a working paper prepared by Charles H. Elliott. Mary G. Powers, Joseph F. Scheuer, Jerome E. McElroy, Selma H. Stevens, and Terrence R. McGovern were responsible for helping to prepare the material from which Chapter 3 on area analysis was written. Jerome McElroy was also the major participant in analyzing data about the East Tremont community used in writing Chapter 4, and, together with Terrence McGovern, collected other community information used in that chapter. Alan L. Grey and Helen E. Dermody prepared a working paper about discontinuities in correctional casework used in writing a section of Chapter 5. Finally, a significant doctoral dissertation on urban lower-class subcultures by Madeline H. Engel provided an important source of material cited in Chapter 1 on the sociogenic case method. If we have failed to report accurately the efforts of these individuals, the responsibility is ours alone. Working across disciplines is always difficult. Writing a book which strives to integrate and present in an orderly form the results of several years' research by a multidisciplinary team is at best a hazardous task.

Many agency people cooperated closely with the authors and their university colleagues. Among those most involved were John F. Hennessy, Chairman, Lincoln Hall Board of Managers, and Brother Augustine Loes, F.S.C., former Director of Lincoln Hall and present Provincial of the New York District of the Christian Brothers. Their patience, support, and persistent efforts to change Lincoln Hall's conventional approach to delinquency are understood and appreciated, as is the difficulty of the task. The radical reform of correctional institutions has never been easy; seldom has it met with marked success. From the public sector, several people deserve special thanks. These include the Honorable Florence M. Kelley, Administrative Judge, Family Court of the State of New York Within the City of New York; John A. Wallace, Director, and Marion M. Brennan and C. Boyd McDivitt, Deputy Directors, of the Office of Probation for the Courts of New York City. These four public officials represented their respective organizations within the structure of the Juvenile Court Community Development Project in which the Family Court and the Office of Probation were participants.

Several of our colleagues read and commented upon the final draft of this book. Wherever possible we have responded to their suggestions, particularly those offered by Steven M. David, Theodore N. Ferdinand, Morris Herman, and Ralph M. Susman.

Among the office staff, Elinor Seery must get particular thanks. She typed most of what went into the various working papers prepared during the past three years. She also played a central role in keeping intact by telephone and mail an essentially part-time professional team. Eileen Kolenik contributed significantly by typing earlier drafts of the manuscript.

Finally, we acknowledge the ever-encouraging support provided by two tolerant wives, Thelma G. Martin and Lois Benjamin Gould, who, believing in the value of work, graced the manuscript with last-stage editorial touches.

J.M.M. / J.P.F. / R.E.G.

January, 1969

contents

the analysis
of delinquent
behavior

INTRODUCTION

A revolution is stirring in national thinking about crime and delinquency. Instead of the old emphasis on changing the individual offender, the new movement stresses changing the manner in which various social institutions, including courts and correctional agencies, relate to him. The causes of delinquency and youth crime in particular are sought in conditions of social and political inequality, especially in lack of economic and educational opportunity, rather than solely in individual pathology and personal failure. The dysfunctional consequences of bureaucratic decisions and practices for the disadvantaged are being given much closer scrutiny. Leaders of the new movement are likely to take their guiding principles from social science and law, as well as psychology. They see that the need to reform social institutions through community action and to win fair decisions for the poor is just as important as therapy, casework, and counseling for individual offenders.

While closely linked historically to reform movements of the past,[1] the new revolution is barely ten years old. Its existence is well known among professionals committed to the cause of meaningful action against crime and delinquency. Of course not all who recognize it accept the validity of its arguments; not all who understand its rationale accept its liberal ideology. Nevertheless, despite periodic reversals and deflections, the movement grows. Agencies are slowly decentralizing in order to get closer to the people they serve. Community-oriented programs are becoming widely accepted. Citizen participation in agency policy-making is occurring more frequently, as is the direct involvement of citizens in on-going programs. New issues regarding citizenship rights and due process are continually being raised; advocacy measures are being discussed and implemented.

Crucial influences on the movement's development during the early 1960s were the reform efforts of the Ford Foundation's "gray area projects" and the various projects launched by the President's Committee on Juvenile Delinquency and Youth Crime in cooperation with the Office of Juvenile Delinquency and Youth Development, both of which were created early in the Kennedy Administration.[2] Fostered by the emerging civil rights movement and later by the nation's War on Poverty, community action and legal representation are now seen as a most efficacious means for easing the problems of disadvantaged groups. Recent responses to collective injustice have been more militant, even deadly. And a great social movement has emerged over resistance to the war in Vietnam. Measured against this global issue, alleviating the problems of the nation's poor seems a reasonable domestic stance. However, institutional reform to meet domestic social problems remains one of the most controversial of questions, the solution of which will affect the future of American democracy.

One of the most significant recent influences forging this revised view of how society should curb crime and delinquency was the President's Commission on Law Enforcement and Administration of Justice, which reported early in 1967.[3] Mandated to map sweeping reforms of national policy in the area of crime prevention and control, the commission sought to stir greater awareness of social and political inequalities suffered by disadvantaged groups and to spur the development of programs for more efficient law enforcement and justice. Throughout the various reports of the commission, community forces and conflicts emerge as central influences in crime and delinquency causation. Throughout the reports there are constant references to gross inequities that have worked their way into the nation's police, judicial, and correctional systems. The challenge of actually introducing into these systems a new environmental emphasis and a concern for safeguarding social and political equality lies ahead. The problems are massive; the dilemmas, many. None is easily resolved. A central difficulty is that of introducing into law enforcement and the administration of justice a real, not hypothetical, balance of power between individuals who are on the receiving end of justice and the officials who administer it. The crucial task will be that of building a public policy which both recognizes and understands the inherent conflicts of interest between those groups and collectivities in society against which the law is enforced and those in whose name and for whose benefit it is enforced.

This book and its companion case-study volume are concerned with only one technical aspect of the much larger problem. Both set forth the main dimensions of a new diagnostic, or assessment, methodology for use in the study of juvenile delinquency. Courts, psychiatric clinics, correctional agencies, police juvenile bureaus, and other public and private delinquency prevention and control agencies adopting this methodology would gain both greater objectivity and deeper understanding in making case and policy decisions about the adolescents and youth with whom they deal. Similarly, minority-group organizations and legal service programs for the disadvantaged will find the new methodology useful as a source of data for influencing decision and policy makers, as these programs and organizations seek greater "justice for the child" coming before law enforcement and criminal justice agencies.

The new methodology, focused sharply on delinquency rather than on crime in general, takes a structural view of causation and seeks to introduce at the individual case level an interdisciplinary, or perhaps more precisely, a multidisciplinary, perspective with a heavy social science emphasis. This emphasis permits a sharp scrutiny of the various structural inequalities that affect the lives and behavior of individual offenders. Combining the traditions of social science with those of psychology, the methodology seeks to reveal, in the biographical sense, the full environmental field within which the delinquent developed as a person; this environmental field itself is then examined, along with all its relationships to the particular delinquent acts that offenders commit. More specifically, the method links the study of biography with the study of history within the context of the delinquent's contemporary community. The focus is on the interrelationships between the delinquent's biography and the history of his people and on the growth, development, and contemporary characteristics of the community in which he and his family live. The configuration of events and social interactions characteristic of the immediate action situations in which the delinquent behavior occurred receives special attention.

The essential problem is first to "see" delinquency—both as isolated acts and as patterned behavior—in terms of the total context within which it occurs and then to link this context to the functioning personalities of individual delinquents.[4] Good examples of "seeing" the human condition in this manner abound in the social science literature. Thus, in his book, *Slavery*,[5] Stanley Elkins provides a classic illustration of the link between social structure and personality. Here Elkins analyzes what he calls the modal "Sambo-like" Negro personality type of the slave era in America and shows how this type arose neither from the "innate nature" of the slave nor from his African culture but rather as a direct consequence of the absolute power of white over black in the American slave system.

Another illustration is provided by Christian Gauss in his introduction to the Mentor edition of Machiavelli's *The Prince*.[6] Gauss clearly demonstrates that Machiavelli and his classic work, rigorously condemned by some, were not at all atypical of the troubled and unstable political climate of fifteenth- and sixteenth-century Florence. As Gauss notes, *The Prince* is a bitter book, written by a man whose reward for his efforts to improve the lot of his country was exile. But this bitterness, born of failure, should not blind us to the value of the book even

today or lead us to overlook Gauss' point that Machiavelli be-
haved as he did in order to be relevant to his historical time and
place.

Countless modern novels also show the value of structural
analysis. Budd Schulberg, in *What Makes Sammy Run?*[7] makes
Sammy Glick understandable as he shoves his way from the
slums of the Lower East Side of New York to the heights of
Hollywood success by presenting Sammy within the context of,
and against the background of, the decade of the 1930s in
America. We may not like Sammy, but we understand him because we also see him in relation to his time and place.

Similarly, Edwin O'Connor, in *The Last Hurrah*,[8] creates
the vivid character of Frank Skeffington, a successful Irish political boss in the Boston of earlier days, a city torn by religious,
social, economic, and political conflicts between the entrenched
Yankee and the Irish newcomer. Skeffington struggles to the top,
struts as king of the hill, and, finally, sees his political power
ebbing away. Again, we may or may not like Skeffington, but we
certainly understand him because we see him in relation to his
time and circumstances.

Machiavelli, Sammy Glick, Frank Skeffington (in anybody's terms, an awesome trio), were not random choices to
show how the social structure can be related to the individual
case. Judged in the light of contemporary values, each one of the
three in a special sense could be considered "delinquent." Even
in their own day some center of power or some source of judgment defined each as deviant. Machiavelli was sent into political
exile, the real-life Skeffington was sent to prison, and nobody at
all seemed able to tolerate the fictional character of Sammy
Glick.

Hence, just as it illuminates and explains the behavior of
these three men, the method of structural analysis offers equally
revealing insights about the behavior of present-day delinquent
children and youths. The study of biography linked with the
study of history within the context of contemporary society is
necessary if the individual delinquent is to be fairly and fully
studied and assessed. The application and further development

of this assessment methodology would thus lead courts, psychiatric clinics, correctional institutions, and other social agencies to a better understanding of the individuals brought to their official and professional attention. Rigorously applied under the tenets of a scientific theory and methodology, the structural approach should help investigators understand more fully what delinquency is all about and what, in social policy and program planning terms, can best be done about it.

The orientation presented here attempts to specify in concrete case terms an interdisciplinary approach to the study of delinquent behavior, applying structural analysis to the study of such deviancy. The original outline of this orientation was reported by John Martin and Joseph Fitzpatrick in their book, *Delinquent Behavior*.[9] Since its publication, some experience has been gained with the orientation in several research, demonstration, and program planning projects undertaken between 1965 and 1968. The results of this experience, plus the original statement of the perspective published in the 1965 book, form the basis of what follows.

This perspective on delinquency may be briefly summarized:

A prevailing emphasis on delinquency as a problem of personality defect, psychic or otherwise, has led society to neglect important structural conditions, both social and cultural, which are most relevant to an understanding of such behavior. Especially neglected have been efforts to take such conditions into account in the study of individual cases. Perhaps the best-known studies of delinquents done from a structural perspective are those by Clifford Shaw,[10] completed more than a generation ago. Quite different from the many available case studies of delinquents, which either implicitly or explicitly have sought to employ some form of psychoanalytic theory, Shaw's work stressed cultural analysis applied to the individual offender. However, it is important to note that Shaw made little use of social organizational variables in his studies of offenders. Nor did he successfully link his form of structural analysis to a psychological view of personality, thus neglecting significant individual differences. For Shaw, personality seemed to be essentially the subjective side of culture.

Edwin Sutherland also put great stress upon social learning in his study of offenders, particularly in his classic study of the professional thief[11] and subsequently in his theory of "differential association," [12] which evolved in the late 1930s and 1940s. Following the tradition of the Chicago School, in which Shaw was also a most significant figure, Sutherland approached personality in highly cultural terms.

Recent studies have been more successful in relating structural variables to personal functioning in explaining behavioral differences among individuals. One of the best-known studies is William Whyte's *Street Corner Society*.[13] Here Whyte provides a significant illustration of how structural analysis in both its social and cultural aspects can be used to explain differences in individual behavior and performance. For example, his analysis points out how role performance in a bowling league was influenced by group expectations, or how, in structural terms, "college boys" differed from "corner boys." But even Whyte's work, milestone though it is, does not attempt to deal with individual differences in the psychological sense in accounting for differences in individual behavior.

Within the last few years additional studies have pushed structural analysis ever closer to that of personality analysis in examining the behavior of individual adolescents, delinquent or otherwise. One of the best of these studies was conducted by Muzafer and Carolyn Sherif,[14] who concluded, after extensive field investigations, that the behavior of the individual adolescent is the result of "interacting influences coming from the individual himself, from his reference groups, and from his sociocultural setting."

Robert Gould's work is representative of a newer psychiatric approach to the problems of delinquency. His "Delinquent Adolescent" [15] indicates how a psychiatrist trained in psychoanalytic and sociocultural methodology uses several disciplines to offer a broader base for understanding delinquent behavior.

The present work is in the "field theory" tradition subscribed to by many well-known social and behavioral scientists. In applying this tradition, it places particular emphasis on the various social action situations in which delinquency occurs and upon the definitions of these situations held by various participants and observers. But the book is also intended to do much more. First, it is a progress report of a continuing effort to build the study of individual cases of delinquent behavior upon a rapidly emerging interdisciplinary knowledge base which embodies a strong structural emphasis. In carrying out this emphasis, effort is made to relate delinquency—both its causes as well as what is done about it—to the organization of the total urban community, including the nature and consequences of the community's political arrangements. Second, in demonstrating the structural roots of delinquency, the intention is to influence public policy makers toward a greater acceptance and use of this perspective in their efforts to frame action programs designed to deal with this form of deviant behavior. Third, in conjunction with *Delinquent Behavior*: *A Redefinition of the Problem* and *Case Studies in the Analysis of Delinquent Behavior,* this book is designed to provide basic educational materials around which courses and in-service training sessions in universities and action agencies can be developed for the teaching of a structural approach to the analysis of delinquent behavior.

Students in sociology and other behavioral sciences may be interested in this approach from a strictly scientific point of view —that is, as an exercise in theory and methodology. Professional personnel in such fields as social work and psychiatry should be interested in the material because of the implications it has for their work roles as they relate to the delinquency question. Development of a competence among such professionals to carry out a new assessment model of the type suggested here would seem essential before any public policy change in the direction of structurally oriented programs in the delinquency field can actually be implemented and realized. The successful application of the new assessment model by social workers, psychiatrists, and others concerned with delinquency will be no easy task. A type of field research not usually undertaken by such professionals will have to be incorporated as part of their work roles. In addition, the social control functions of these professionals as they usually relate to delinquents will have to be circumvented in a manner that does not compromise the professional either with delinquents or the agency by which he is employed.[16]

The new model holds that delinquency is not exclusively, or even necessarily, symptomatic of some individual personality defect, psychic or otherwise. Following the classic culture-conflict line of structural analysis, for example, the label "delinquency" may often be evoked to describe behavior which, condemned by the dominant society, occasions official action but which may otherwise be defined as culturally normative behavior in the social, ethnic, or other subgroup to which the "delinquent" belongs. A case illustration from the research carried out in preparation for writing this book will serve to clarify this point.

Pedro F.* was first brought to court by his mother when he was thirteen. The mother complained that she could not control Pedro, that he was truant and, when in school, a behavior problem. He later appeared in the same court on several other occasions: once for carrying a weapon to school; once for threatening a teacher with whom he was having a fight; and once for threatening another boy with a knife after an aborted street gang fight.

While under correctional care, Pedro's sexual activities also came under scrutiny. When he was thirteen, he began living in his first consensual union—that is, living together without marriage; his first child was lost by miscarriage when he was fourteen; his second child was born when he was sixteen; at seventeen, he was beginning his second consensual union with a girl who was already pregnant by him.

Correctional authorities responded to this boy in various

---

* This boy and some of the other adolescents cited throughout this book are described more completely in a companion volume of case studies, *Case Studies in the Analysis of Delinquent Behavior*, also to be published by Random House.

ways, usually negative. He was described as a "vicious and immoral young man," as "seriously disturbed emotionally," as
"showing no signs of remorse," as "continually resisting involving himself in a casework relationship," as having an "extremely
warped personality," and finally and most blatantly as "a sonofabitch who again 'knocked up' a girl." A training school psychiatrist described him as having "lived according to the morals of
the gang and [of being] more dyssocial than asocial."

Pedro's many friends, his consensual partners, and some of
his own extended family liked the youth. They understood that
his consensual unions were very much the same as their own and
in the tradition of the kind of people they came from in Puerto
Rico. Pedro and his people were farm people, of a type known
as stubborn *jibaros*. In their section of Puerto Rico, consensual
union was a fairly common practice. *Jibaros* are a people used
to hardships, with a toughness needed to cope with life as they
experience it. In time of trouble the family is the primary re-
source. Neither law, nor institutions, nor formal organizations
are the pillars on which the securities of life are based, but
rather the brother, the friend, the *compadre*. Their watchword
is, "When I call, they come no matter what the cost." Pedro and
his people brought this life style with them when they migrated
to New York City. In their Lower East Side neighborhood,
Pedro became one of the most significant adolescents around.
There he was looked upon as loyal and *guapo*—that is, tough,
courageous, a fighter.

The culture conflict between the life style to which Pedro
belonged and that of middle-class American norms is most evident in this case synopsis. The conflict is further highlighted by
the descriptions of Pedro given by various correctional authorities while he was under their care. "Vicious and immoral," an
"extremely warped personality," "a sonofabitch," and other
such expressions all put the question in a highly individualized
way, as if society were unanimously agreed about what was
"right" and what was "wrong" and as if Pedro for personal reasons alone had violated society's standards. Even the clinical use
of the term "dyssocial," although it conveys some idea of the

group support Pedro received for his behavior, misses in a technical and analytical sense the cultural nature of this support. It fails to convey an understanding of both the *relative* and especially the *functional* nature of all social norms,[17] even those of Pedro, his family, and his friends. To describe Pedro as "dyssocial" implies that the "morals" to which he subscribed were themselves dysfunctional. Thus this term overlooks the fact that social norms which may be dysfunctional when seen from the point of view of the more established sectors of society are often *highly* functional when seen from the perspective and interests of the subgroup or subcommunity subscribing to such norms.

Thus Pedro's behavior, which society deemed delinquent, followed expected cultural patterns, which were normative according to the behavioral standards set by the groups to which he belonged.

The marked discrepancy, or more precisely the conflict, between the authorities' view of Pedro and that of his friends and relatives, is in itself an interesting phenomenon. This conflict goes to the heart of any attempt to understand what Pedro is like, what precisely he did or did not do, why he did or did not do it, and, most significant, how harshly he should be judged because of his behavior. For example, at several points in his correctional career, several workers who had come into contact with Pedro on the supervisory, as opposed to the professional, level, considered him to be a good worker, a "cool" adolescent who knew how to handle himself physically, but who quietly stayed out of trouble.

However, these impressions found no conspicuous place in the official case material available about the youth. Systematic treatment of these and other positive impressions Pedro made on at least some of the authority figures with whom he came into contact would have done much to counter the almost entirely negative assessments various correctional psychiatrists and social caseworkers made of the youth and reported in his official case records.

Erving Goffman makes a similar point in his comments about the written records kept on state hospital patients and other inmates of "total institutions." [18] When authorities write about individuals in trouble, they almost invariably seem to describe them as troublesome individuals.

This pattern emerged repeatedly in the intensive case investigations done in preparation for writing this book. When official records present blatant moral judgments about an adolescent, such as Pedro, it is perhaps to be expected that these judgments be cast negatively. But so strong an accent on the negative by social caseworkers and other clinicians making professional judgments on offenders raises a fundamental question regarding the theoretical biases of many of these practitioners when they come to explain delinquency and to describe individuals who have been adjudged delinquent. It may well be that the stress such professionals put on personal pathology as the sole explanation of delinquency, and the very terminology they use to describe delinquents, colors and otherwise influences their ability to perceive and to portray offenders more objectively. This bias is perhaps reinforced by the manner in which the professional in corrections carries out his work role. Office interviews in the courthouse, training school, or other agency setting are much favored over extensive field interviews and intimate contact with the offender, his people, and their problems. Besides the adolescent himself, and perhaps his parents, informants are much more often other professionals rather than the offender's friends and frequently numerous relatives. Thus a central thrust in the structural view of delinquency presented here is the introduction of a substantially greater measure of objectivity into the assessment of delinquent adolescents and their behavior.

Culture conflict, exacerbated by profound distortions in the way even highly trained professionals may "see" minority-group and other lower-class delinquents, is therefore a major line of structural analysis employed by the assessment methodology presented here.

A second and most significant structural line of analysis of equal importance in the methodology is that which emphasizes socially induced stress or "tension state" theories in accounting for delinquent behavior. Analysis of this type has become increasingly popular in sociological thinking about delinquency causation ever since Albert Cohen published *Delinquent Boys*[19] in 1955. This perspective was advanced even more significantly by the publication of *Delinquency and Opportunity*[20] in 1960. In essence, this general theory holds that delinquency is a response to frustration as society, holding up for emulation only middle-class ideals, denies to millions of youngsters—by giving them inadequate schools, housing, and employment opportunities—the possibility of realizing these ideals through law-abiding means.

In writing recently of affluence and adolescent crime, Jackson Toby illustrates at the individual case level how youths from several very different affluent countries can get involved in delinquency because of their feelings of material deprivation.[21] In case histories from Japan, Israel, and Sweden, Toby shows how the resentment of poverty, not poverty alone, can cause crime. Thus, Toby concludes, "resentment of poverty is more likely to develop among the relatively deprived of a rich society than among the objectively deprived in a poor society." [22] In still other situations of stress, delinquency may be an expression of racial strife, of the alienation of adolescence, or of other dislocations in the social structure.

To be successful, the methodology presented here must be broad enough in scope to include both culture conflict and socially induced stress lines of analysis in its study of individual cases. To the maximum extent possible, it should also provide for the development of interpretations which, where applicable, permit the two lines of analysis to be combined in a given case or series of cases.

Finally, the methodology strives to take into account both the historical antecedents of given delinquent acts as these are found to be characteristic of both delinquents and their environments, as well as the various "situational" or on-the-spot circumstances which occasioned, or "triggered," a particular act. The method holds that the meaning of an act which the dominant society terms delinquent can be adequately understood only when the full range of social, cultural, situational, *and* personal variables involved have been identified and related to one another. In the light of this information, it may become very clear, for example, that delinquency in a given neighborhood is not simply the acting out of personality defects but rather largely represents patterns of behavior that should realistically be expected, because of cultural or other structural reasons, to occur in that setting. When this is the case, it seems reasonable that, to be effective, any program of intervention should be directed not only toward the personality and familial relationships of individual delinquents, but also toward the social and cultural setting itself.

Concretely, the task is to equip delinquency workers with a perspective that will enable them to consider the full realities of modern life as they relate to the children and youth referred to their care. To be relevant, such workers, for example, must learn how to explain the collective participation of lower-class Negro teen-agers in the racial violence of a Watts, a Detroit, or a Washington, D.C. as clearly as their present casework and clinical abilities can now explain the largely idiosyncratic behavior of a middle-class, white, adolescent Peeping Tom. Once workers have this capacity, then, given the right combination of public support, the way should be open for their development of suitable program alternatives.

The essentials of this new structural orientation, as developed to date, are as follows:

First, the delinquent behavior of a given child or adolescent is best understood in terms of the total *motivational-situational-cultural complexes* within which it occurs. Examination of motivation alone, or of solely the concrete situations in which delinquency occurs, or of merely the cultural components involved in such behavior is insufficient. All must converge in explaining the dependent variable: delinquent behavior. It is important to note that the central object of examination is the delinquent *behavior* of given children and youth, *not* their personalities. The challenge is to link diagnostically the personalities of particular delinquents with the full field of environmental forces, both historical and situational, within which they are operating, in order to understand more fully what they do.[23]

Second, an effective perspective for understanding such complexes is a comprehensive interdisciplinary theory of delinquency causation in which the central integrating theme emphasizes not only the psychic aspect, but also the social and cultural aspects, of human behavior. Following in the field theory tradition of Clyde Kluckhohn, Henry A. Murray, Harry Stack Sullivan, and others, sharp emphasis is placed on the interrelationships among environmental influences, personality, and behavior, with special concern shown for embracing the widest possible range of social and cultural variables.

Third, in applying such an interdisciplinary perspective to the study of an individual case, it is necessary to use such social science concepts as "social class," "subculture," "reference groups," "status and role," "attitudes," "values," "norms," and similar analytical tools. Through the bridge provided by the disciplines of social psychology and relevant psychiatry, the social and cultural forces acting upon an individual delinquent must be linked to the particular delinquent act he commits in meeting particular situations within his special milieu.

Finally, three methods of investigation are needed to apply this perspective to the individual case:*

1. *The sociogenic case history,* a method of biographical study which emphasizes the interrelationships among:

   (a) the behavioral patterns, mores, and values characteristic of the various cultural and subcultural systems in which the individual participates;

   (b) the informal social groups (peers, family, and so on) to which the individual belongs and which

---

* For earlier statements regarding the necessity of using a combination of the following methods for the study of delinquent behavior, see Martin and Fitzpatrick, *op. cit.,* pp. 171–176; and John M. Martin, "Case Studies of Delinquents: Incorporating the Sociological Approach," *Social Work* 4:16–22 (October 1959).

serve to structure his most intimate social relationships;

(c) the formal institutional structures to which the individual relates or fails to relate (school, community center, church, and so on) and the nature and
quality of the specific relationships involved;

(d) personality variables which must be evaluated in
each individual in terms of his *particular* experience
in the context of a, b, and c, described above. These
variables are his personal and socially shared attitudes, values, norms, and so on, his status frustrations and other consequences of socially induced
stress, and his possible psychopathology. With respect to the last, the crucial considerations are:
Does psychopathology exist in the individual? If
so, is it related to his delinquent acts? If it is, how
is it related?

2. *Situational analysis,** which focuses sharply on delinquent acts, the immediate situations in which they occur,
and on sorting out the meaning such acts have at three
levels of interpretation:

(a) the dominant cultural level represented by middle-
class values, norms, and interpretations of delinquent behavior as these are applied to the delinquent by such functionaries as school teachers, the

---

* This method regards deviancy, including delinquency, as the result of
a process of social interaction between those who are defined as deviants and those who do the defining. This is in contrast to the more
conventional approach which has for so long focused on the deviant
himself and his characteristics. A good discussion of this point is found
in Howard S. Becker, ed., *The Other Side: Perspectives on Deviance*.
New York: Free Press, 1964, pp. 2–4. The method also acknowledges
the fact that most *official* delinquents appear to come from the lower
class and from various disadvantaged groups, depending upon the particular historical period and community from which the cases originate.
When delinquents are from the middle class, situational analysis requires that strict attention be paid to identifying, describing, and comparing relevant subcultural differences within that group.

police, judges, probation officers, correctional psychiatrists and psychologists, and other officials who
deal with the delinquent on a face-to-face basis;
(b) the lower-class and minority-group subcultural
level to which the delinquent's family belongs;
(c) the peer-reference group level to which the delinquent belongs.
3. The *area analysis* (or *epidemiological*) method, which
identifies and describes areas of high delinquency concentration within the context of changing urban communities. To achieve this end, the method utilizes the techniques of demography, ecology, urban history, and
social work community organization.

Working together in the development and application of
these three methods, members of an interdisciplinary team included sociologists specializing in both organizational and cultural lines of analysis, demographers, a social psychologist, a
psychiatrist, clinical psychologists, social caseworkers, and spe-
cialists in community organization. At first one case, then two
cases, for intensive analysis were selected from Lincoln Hall, a
private training school taking court-committed cases largely
from New York City. One youth lived in Queens and the other
in Manhattan, two of the city's five boroughs. It soon became
apparent, however, that the efficiency of the three methods as
used together would be greatly increased if the cases studied
were all drawn from the same neighborhood. Selecting cases in
this manner accomplished two objectives. One, the method of
area analysis, which requires extensive demographic and field
investigation to ascertain the characteristics of the neighborhood
in which the action in a single case unfolds, would not have to
be repeated for different neighborhoods if all the cases studied in
a series came from the same neighborhood. Two, in examining a
number of different cases from the same neighborhood by means
of the sociogenic case method and the method of situational
analysis, it became clear that an in-depth understanding of the
neighborhood itself was developing progressively with the com-

pletion of each case. This approach also yielded deeper insight into the relationships among the adolescents studied, as well as a more complete grasp of their relationships to those organizational and cultural components in their neighborhood significant for an understanding of their behavior.

In sum, selecting cases from the same neighborhood simplified matters considerably; moreover, it made possible a clearer understanding of the adolescents themselves and their relationships one to another, the locale in which they operated, and their places within it. Eventually nine adolescents from the East Tremont section of the Bronx, in New York City, were intensively studied in this manner. At the time of selection, all were living in this area while on probation from the Family Court.

The orientation and assessment methodology did not consider these cases in isolation from one another. The cases were first each studied individually, and then they were studied *collectively*. This permitted diagnostically relevant patterns to emerge and links between individual cases to be perceived. It also facilitated demonstration of the relationship between individual case data and prevailing environmental conditions. Most significant, however, it directed attention to the local environment itself as an object of investigation. Used in this fashion, the individual delinquents studied, as well as the various local people interviewed in preparing the case studies, served as informants, not only about themselves but also about local conditions. Each case study done in this manner served as a sort of "small window" into a milieu which might otherwise have proved extremely difficult for the investigators to penetrate. Experience with this methodology suggests that when even a few cases from a given area are studied in this manner, a great deal can be learned, not only about the central figures in the different case studies, but also about their interrelationships and about their milieu or neighborhood.

This methodological procedure is vital for advancing a structural approach to the study of delinquency. Once the focus is broadened from a preoccupation with the individual and his family to include delinquents as collectivities, as well as their environments, a whole new range of etiological variables may be brought into play, at both the level of the larger society and at the level of the "operating milieu." [24] These variables are not ordinarily considered by existing diagnostic practices. At the same time, because the delinquent and his family[25] are not lost sight of, the multiplicity of variables at these two levels of analysis may also be considered. When all four levels are brought together, individual delinquents are both more clearly distinguishable from one another, in terms of the etiology of their illegal behavior, and more understandable, in terms of the environment within which they operate and to which they respond.

As data for different urban neighborhoods in which official delinquents are concentrated are developed and assessed according to this new method of analysis, environmental variations should become more clearly delineated in diagnostic statements about delinquents and their behavior. In addition, structural differences, in the organizational and cultural sense, between different geographic areas of high delinquency concentration—sometimes called slums or ghettos, especially by outsiders—should also become more accurately identified.

Both of these efforts are at present still in their infancy: the work roles of professionals in diagnostic and social agencies concerned with delinquency now rarely address themselves to these problems. The education of psychiatrists, psychologists, and social workers—the key professionals who staff such agencies—does not train these practitioners to scrutinize human behavior from this perspective. The available social science literature that could be called upon to guide work toward these objectives has not been sufficiently refined and adapted so that it can be routinely applied in the concrete situation. Yet the challenge remains and, in fact, grows progressively stronger: *Know the delinquent within the context of his own community; otherwise you don't really know him at all*. This book is offered as a guideline for the achievement of such understanding.

Chapter 1 presents the sociogenic case method "model" used in the analysis of all the cases studied in the course of the research. Chapter 2 sets forth the method of situational analysis used in these case analyses. The procedures by which the East Tremont section of the Bronx was selected as the research locale, as well as some of the demographic, ecological, and other characteristics of that area and the Bronx itself over time, are described in Chapter 3. Chapter 4 discusses at length the question of power in the delinquency field as it relates to the manner in which delinquency is defined, who defines it, how public decisions about this form of deviancy are made, and who makes them. The chapter also presents the results obtained in the East Tremont section, a neighborhood which during the research was undergoing rapid social change, when the three methods—the sociogenic case history, situational analysis, and area analysis— were combined for the structural analysis of delinquent behavior. Finally, Chapter 5 considers briefly some of the policy implications of the new perspective as it relates to major contemporary issues in the delinquency field. This chapter also suggests in a preliminary way some new strategies for agency functioning and new work roles for agency personnel as communities learn to view delinquency from a structural point of view.

References

1. For a historical treatment of the persistence of an opportunity theme in American social reform, see Eric F. Goldman, *Rendezvous with Destiny*. New York: Vintage Books, 1956.

2. For a discussion of these two influences and their underlying assumptions, see Peter Marris and Martin Rein, *Dilemmas of Social Reform: Poverty and Community Action in the United States*. New York: Atherton Press, 1967.

3. A summary of the various policy recommendations made by this commission is found in *The Challenge of Crime in a Free Society*. Washington, D.C.: Government Printing Office, February 1967.

4. An earlier statement about the need for studying social behavior

from such a perspective was made by C. Wright Mills in *The Sociological Imagination*. New York: Oxford University Press, 1959.

5. Stanley M. Elkins, *Slavery: A Problem in American Institutional and Intellectual Life*. New York: Grosset & Dunlap, 1963.

6. Niccolo Machiavelli, *The Prince*. New York: Mentor edition, New American Library of World Literature, 1952.

7. Budd Schulberg, *What Makes Sammy Run?* New York: Bantam, 1961.

8. Edwin O'Connor, *The Last Hurrah*. Boston: Little, Brown, 1956.

9. John M. Martin and Joseph P. Fitzpatrick, *Delinquent Behavior: A Redefinition of the Problem*. New York: Random House, 1965, especially Chap. 5.

10. Clifford R. Shaw, *The Jack-roller*. Chicago: University of Chicago Press, 1930; Clifford R. Shaw, *The Natural History of a Delinquent Career*. Chicago: University of Chicago Press, 1931; and Clifford R. Shaw, *Brothers in Crime*. Chicago: University of Chicago Press, 1938.

11. Edwin H. Sutherland, *The Professional Thief*. Chicago: University of Chicago Press, 1937.

12. See, e.g., Edwin H. Sutherland, *Principles of Criminology*. Philadelphia: Lippincott, 1939. Sutherland modified his theory in the 1947 edition of this text and it has remained unchanged through the 1966 edition by Sutherland and Donald R. Cressey.

13. William F. Whyte, *Street Corner Society*. Chicago: University of Chicago Press, 1943.

14. Muzafer Sherif and Carolyn W. Sherif, *Reference Groups: Exploration into Conformity and Deviation of Adolescents*. New York: Harper & Row, 1964.

15. Robert E. Gould, "The Delinquent Adolescent," in Sol Nichtern, ed., *Mental Health Services for Adolescents: Proceedings of the Second Hillside Hospital Conference*. New York: Frederick A. Praeger, 1968, Chap. 17.

16. A further discussion of these and related points is provided in Ned Polsky, *Hustlers, Beats, and Others*. Chicago: Aldine Publishing, 1967, Chap. 3.

17. For a further discussion of this point, which is pivotal for an understanding of a structural approach to the analysis of delinquent behavior, see Martin and Fitzpatrick, *op. cit.*, Chap. 1.

18. Erving Goffman, *Asylums*. Garden City, N.Y.: Anchor Books, Doubleday, 1961, especially pp. 84 ff., 154 ff., and 374 ff.

19. Albert K. Cohen, *Delinquent Boys: The Culture of the Gang*. New York: Free Press, 1955.

20. Richard A. Cloward and Lloyd E. Ohlin, *Delinquency and Opportunity*. New York: Free Press, 1960.

21. Jackson Toby, "Affluence and Adolescent Crime," in *Task Force Report: Juvenile Delinquency and Youth Crime*. The President's Commission on Law Enforcement and Administration of Justice. Washington, D.C.: Government Printing Office, 1967, pp. 132–144.

22. *Ibid.*, p. 143.

23. A good recent statement of this general perspective is provided in J. Milton Yinger, *Toward a Field Theory of Behavior*. New York: McGraw-Hill, 1965.

24. For a discussion of these two levels, see Martin and Fitzpatrick, *op. cit.*, Chaps. 2 and 3.

25. See *ibid.*, Chap. 4, for a discussion of these two levels.

Chapter 1

THE SOCIOGENIC
CASE METHOD

The Theory of the Sociogenic
Case History

The interdisciplinary method for the study of delinquency described in the Introduction begins with the sociogenic case history. This is a biographical method that seeks to gather all the necessary social, cultural, and social psychological data through which the life history of the youth may be reviewed in clear perspective and to examine the delinquent act which the youth committed in the context of this life history. The method also provides the context and perspective in which the personality can be examined in the light of a wide range of historical experiences that have helped to form it and in which the relationship of personality variables to social and cultural variables can be more accurately identified.

The essential task is to relate in logical fashion well-defined causes to the particular misbehavior of particular children acting to solve their problems within specific motivational-situational-cultural complexes. Only then can we judge the relevance of different social, cultural, or personal theories of causation. Only then can we decide on the kinds of action most likely to be effective in the prevention and control of delinquency.[1]

Figure 1 presents the interdisciplinary scheme for the study of all the variables mentioned above and their interrelationship. The sociogenic case history involves the study of the Independent and the Intervening Variables and the Dependent Variable, summarized as follows from Martin and Fitzpatrick: [2]

Independent Variables are of two kinds: (1) social and cultural background items, such as social class, ethnic, family, and neighborhood characteristics; and (2) physical properties of the individual human organism, such as age, sex, skin color, and intelligence, many of which take on meaning only in a cultural context. Each of the two kinds of variables is related to the other by the total processes of personality growth and development set forth in applicable behavioral and social science theories. The sociogenic case history emphasizes the social psychological theories of human learning and conditioning developed by social scientists. Most important are theories of socialization[3] and theories of socially induced personality stress.[4]

Intervening Variables are of three classes: (1) the first class consists of attitudes, values, motives, and other definitions either acquired by the actor from others through socialization and other aspects of social learning or developed idiosyncratically and privately; (2) the second class consists of different forms of socially induced personality strain or tension states as these originate in structured strain experienced by the actor in terms of the social organizations and groups in which he participates (A source of these may be family life or participation in the violent, chaotic, tension-ridden subworlds such as are found in disorganized slums of large cities); and (3) the third class consists of personality traits deeply rooted in the unconscious and reflecting different degrees of mental illness or personality disorder. All three classes are rooted in the interplay of background variables and relevant properties of the organism. Intervening Variables are predispositions to act or not to act, which the actor brings with him to the delinquent action situation.

Figure 1. INTERDISCIPLINARY SCHEME

INDEPENDENT VARIABLES	INTERVENING VARIABLES	DEPENDENT VARIABLE

Social-Cultural Background—e.g., social class, ethnic, and minority status; family structural, cultural, and behavioral characteristics; structure and culture of neighborhood; community status along "good boy"—"bad boy" continuum; school achievement; gang membership

(Relevant parts of theoretical levels I, II, and III)

Process of personality growth and development, including socialization

Properties of the Organism—e.g., age, sex, skin color, intelligence, physical size, deformities, organic mental disease

(Relevant parts of theoretical level IV)

Three Classes:

(1) Personal and socially shared attitudes, values, motives, norms; self-definition along "good boy"—"bad boy" continuum

(2) Status frustrations and other socially induced strains

(3) Psychotic and neurotic reactions, character disorders, and related mental disturbances

(Relevant parts of theoretical level IV, excluding those listed under Independent Variables, belong in this column)

The "Feedback" Effect of Delinquent Acts —each experienced by an actor, becomes part of his on-going life experience*

Problem-Solving Situations: **Delinquent Act****

Described in terms of their historical, social, and cultural contexts, especially in terms of "culture conflict" and intergroup and interpersonal conflict

(Relevant parts of theoretical levels I, II, III, and IV)

*Each experience involves the "satisfactions," both conscious and unconscious, received by the actor from having committed his delinquent act as balanced off against the "negative consequences" his act has for him. The latter range all the way from the actor's finding out that a particular delinquent solution "doesn't work" to his experiencing the stigmatizing influences of becoming a case for law enforcement and correctional agencies.

**For example, truancy, theft, assault, vandalism, or street-gang murder. (Each delinquent act to be analyzed in terms of the "action frame of reference"—means-ends-conditions-norms)

Source: John M. Martin and Joseph P. Fitzpatrick, *Delinquent Behavior: A Redefinition of the Problem.* New York: Random House, 1965, p. 165.

The Dependent Variable is the behavior to be explained, a particular delinquent act—for example, a theft or an assault. The central fact to be explained is action in a situation. The Dependent Variable is therefore directly studied by the method of situational analysis, which will be explained in Chapter 2. However, the pre-existing mental sets of the actor are considered as Intervening Variables in the scheme. As such, they are viewed as personality traits of the actor, traits which he "carries around" with him as he encounters one social situation after another through life. The sociogenic case history seeks to discover the significant factors, cultural or social, in the background of the actor, which have contributed to a particular tendency to act in one way or another. It seeks to understand the personality of the present by a study of the influences on the personality in the past; it studies the actor in terms of those factors in his development which best explain him as part of an action situation.

"The Feedback Effect of Delinquent Acts" must also be considered. Once a delinquent act is engaged in, it "feeds back" as part of the life experience of the actor to become itself an influence in his personality growth and development. In terms of the scheme, an actor's experiences with the Dependent Variable cross back and, as background items, function as Independent Variables leading to new or reinforced Intervening Variables (predispositions to act). In other words, the act may have "worked" or "not worked," in a problem-solving sense; it may have been satisfying or dissatisfying; it may or may not have left the actor branded as a "bad boy." Any of these experiences may have fed back into the continuing development of the actor's life. In this sense, the sociogenic case history directs particular attention to the actor's life development as thus understood. In studying the actor in this way, in terms of social-psychological theories of development, and in emphasizing the interplay of social and cultural background items with the physical properties of the organism as significant influences on a person's disposition to act, the sociogenic case history is a distinct departure from the psychogenic case study method which has been customary in social and psychiatric services in recent generations.

The psychogenic case study emphasizes the understanding of behavior on the basis of unconscious factors influencing it. According to this method, the roots of personality development and its warps are looked for primarily in the relationships of the infant and growing child to the significant figures in his life, usually his parents or parent-surrogates. The type and degree and time sequence of these relationships are given close attention in the overall evaluation of the personality makeup and in the understanding of behavior patterns.

Experiences of a traumatic nature, whether these have occurred occasionally or constantly as a "way of life," tend to be repressed so that the person avoids feeling anxiety associated with such unpleasant experiences. Repressed material, under certain circumstances, emerges as a series of "symptoms" of a maladaptive way of life—a "character disorder" or, if severe, a "psychosis."

The psychogenic case study attempts to uncover the unconscious material and to reveal the conflicts that have contributed to a particular behavior pattern. With this method, the therapist sets the stage for "working through" these conflicts by helping the individual to understand their origins. The theory holds that exposing the defenses or security operations employed to deny entry of conflicts from the unconscious mind to consciousness, and achieving insight into the nature of these conflicts, opens the door to change.

The sociogenic case history accepts the validity of this psychogenic method. However, the sociogenic case method addresses itself directly to the personality in terms of its social-psychological development; it focuses on personal and socially shared values, motives, and norms and on status frustrations and other socially induced strains. Within this context, the sociogenic case history then studies the personality psychogenically. It tends to emphasize the personality primarily as an expression of the particular culture to which a person belongs, a manifestation of norms and patterns of expected behavior within that culture. Sociogenically, the person is viewed as filling a social role in the presence of historical influences, which, when understood, reveal the meaning of the way he acts. In the study of behavior of a lower-class Negro involved in a rent strike or a school boycott in New York City, for example, the sociogenic method would tend to stress those historical experiences that reveal the behavior to be an act of social protest or part of a strategem aimed at securing better living conditions. It would not tend, as the psychogenic method might, to search primarily for hidden causes suggested by psychoanalytic theory. It is more akin to the approach, based on social learning theory, which Julian Rotter describes in *Clinical Psychology*:

> Another major aspect of social learning theory is the weight it gives to the psychological situation of the individual both in understanding and predicting behavior. In contrast with trait or faculty approaches, or in fact any personality approach that places all the stress on internal states, this view, because of its basic learning theory assumptions, emphasizes that an individual learns through past experiences that some satisfactions are more likely in some situations than in others. Individual differences exist not only in the strength of different needs but in the way the same situation is perceived. An individual's reactions to different situations depend on his own past experience, which therefore constitutes an important aspect of individual differences. The psychological situation, then, provides the cues for a person's expectancies that his behaviors will lead to desired outcome.[5]

Past social-psychological experiences, therefore, which throw light on the meaning of present acts, are the concern of the sociogenic case method.

For example, Ralph G. is a Puerto Rican youth, sixteen years old, who was brought to court for being involved in the stealing of an automobile. To authority figures, his probation officer, the arresting officer, schoolteachers, and counselors, he appears shy, quiet, halting in speech, confused, and generally uncommunicative. His behavior in his operating milieu is quite different and generally unknown to authorities. He smokes marijuana and buys, rolls, and sells "sticks" for a good profit. He recounts incidents of stealing merchandise in order to sell it at local stores. He wants money and is unhappy without it, and he has mounted a series of modest but lucrative enterprises to keep himself supplied with cash.

The court psychiatrist diagnosed the boy as a "passive-aggressive personality," because he is submissive in the presence of authority and aggressive when out of reach, and the contrasts in the boy's behavior would seem to bear out this "psychogenic" explanation. However, when studied against the background of his family, "sociogenically," the boy's behavior can be understood quite differently. He comes from a family with a long history of involvement in profitable enterprise. On the side of both father and mother, he comes from a tradition of small, industrious shopkeepers who display a strong emphasis on acquiring property through hard work. Ralph appears to be responding to these family patterns of business, of owning property, of being independent in the possession of money. His emphasis on money rather than property may be a translation of family values into terms of his peer group reference system. He is a busy, enterprising, fairly successful entrepreneur in the theft and sale of stolen goods, in the buying and selling of marijuana. In this area, he displays an energy and intelligence quite different from what he displays in school. His ideas about work and money leave no room for recognition of the need for education. His family saw no such need, and neither does he. As he once remarked, going to school keeps him from getting a job. As described in later chapters of the present book, against the background of his neighborhood situation (the East Tremont section of the Bronx), an area characterized by widespread alienation of youth from adults, a lack of legitimate opportunity, and the ready availability of illegal opportunity structures, Ralph's behavior can be seen as the logical application of family traits and traditions. It has the appearance of rational behavior, which it does not appear to have when viewed outside of these perspectives.

The Origin of Case Study Methods

The case history method is in no way new. It was developed and refined in medical practice as doctors recognized that illnesses did not always occur suddenly but that they developed through long or short chains of events. The value of the medical case history was twofold: (1) the study of the history of the development of the illness enabled doctors to diagnose the illness more reliably; and (2) as it became clear that particular illnesses had specific histories, doctors could often arrest an illness in its early stages when they discovered the presence of its historical antecedents. The case history method was later adopted by social welfare workers as casework developed in that profession. The original purpose of the welfare case history seems to have been an effort to distinguish the deserving from the undeserving poor. The history which led to a man's misfortune enabled the social worker to distinguish between those who had fallen into misery through no fault of their own and those who presumably had brought the difficulty upon themselves. Furthermore, the case history enabled the social welfare worker to define more clearly what the difficulty was. The historical experience of a client, for example, could reveal to a social worker that a man's difficulty was really economic rather than medical. Meanwhile, the nature of the case history tended to shift as the purpose of social work shifted. Was social work primarily directed to social reform, personal moral reform, relief of poverty, or the treatment of personality difficulties? As Philip Klein pointed out in 1937, "The very foundation of all social work lies in *a priori* judgments of what is socially desirable and what is not." [6] During the past two generations, social casework has had a strong psychological orientation. It has tended to define the cause of the client's problems in terms of some failure or a maladjustment of the personality. Consequently, social work case histories are generally of the psychogenic type. As indicated above, this often includes a consideration of social and cultural variables such as poverty, unemployment, deprivation, and discrimination. But the clue to action is sought in the subjective tendencies of the individual personality. Simply illustrated, the point of view goes like this: Unemployment leads to a client's frustration, which results in psychic tension, which bursts out in his aggressive behavior. Therapy is directed toward lessening the psychic tension, finding the client a job, or both.

According to the theory on which this book is based, namely, that a delinquent act may proceed from a multiplicity of causes, psychological, cultural, social, and situational, the case history is likewise of central importance, but the emphasis is on sociogenic variables and on understanding psychogenic variables in relation to these. In this way, the psychogenic method itself is considerably modified as the nature of personality involvements in delinquency are more clearly perceived in the light of sociogenic variables. The sociogenic case history seeks to discover the relevant social and cultural experiential factors which contributed to the development of the personality acting in the situation and to relate significant historical factors to the person and the act. It seeks to identify in the life history of the individual those historical variables which have structured for him the perception, attitudes, and stance he has toward his work, his environment, and his behavior. These sets of variables are of two types, cultural and organizational. Variables of the cultural type are those which become related to norms, the patterns of expected behavior, the processes by which an individual is aware he is a member of a social group, sensitive to fundamental definitions of honor, fidelity, generosity, and love. Variables of the organizational type are those related to the associations and institutions which have structured the individual's environment, such as schools, churches, political parties, and business groups.

This does not mean that psychic variables are omitted. Class 3 of the Intervening Variables in Figure 1, namely, psychotic and neurotic reactions, character disorders, and so forth, is of prime interest in the sociogenic case history method. However, the clinical evaluation which seeks to identify and describe these variables is done in the context of the entire range of variables described above. When executed in this manner, the clinical evaluation does not become as central as it generally does in psychogenic case histories. It is but part of a total assessment process in which psychopathological variables, even when they are operative in a given case, are sometimes seen to have little or no relation to the delinquent behavior characteristic of the case.

One of the cases studied in doing the research for this book provides a good illustration. Henry R. was a thirteen-year-old Negro boy, a lower-class, second-generation migrant from the South. When brought to court as a delinquent, he had been engaging in sexual intercourse for about a year. His four older brothers had married (one had begun in a common-law relationship) after their girl friends had become pregnant. Henry's sixteen-year-old sister, married and living at home with her newborn infant, had also been pregnant before marriage.

All the boys in the family had started sexual activity, as had their peers, when they were about thirteen. In the rural South where he came from, the boy's father had had a similar history of early sexual experience; he saw nothing wrong in such activity for boys. He had some reservations about similar behavior for girls, but, insofar as his own daughter was concerned, he really regretted only that she had been "caught," and therefore forced to get married so young. None of his boys felt any guilt or anxiety about their sexual behavior.

Thus, measured by the social standards of his subculture, Henry's delinquent activity—that is, his sexual experience—would appear to be nondeviant behavior and not symptomatic of any personal pathology.

Henry also happened to be of low intelligence and schizophrenic, although not recognized as such by the court. This diagnosis was made by the research psychiatrist and psychologist, on the basis of data which were quite clear-cut and noncontroversial. Yet the chronic schizophrenic process from which Henry suffered was not integrally related to the etiology of his delinquent behavior. These acts were best explained by the cultural characteristics of his life situation. The study of these characteristics may be called the cultural emphasis[7] in sociogenic case histories.

The Cultural Emphasis

The introduction of sociogenic variables into case histories can be conveniently dated from the studies of the Polish peasant[8] conducted by W. I. Thomas and Florian Znaniecki.

The principal sources of data which Thomas and Znaniecki used were the letters exchanged between the immigrants who had come to the United States and their families and friends who had remained in Poland. They also used autobiographies prepared by the immigrants. Subsequently, this study caused continued discussion and controversy about the utilization of these kinds of data in sociological research. However, the data enabled Thomas and Znaniecki to achieve two objectives: (1) documentation of the basic features of the culture of the Polish immigrants; and (2) tracing the development of the problems which arise as people become uprooted from their traditional way of life and face adjustments to a new and different culture. As a result, these authors were the first to bring the concept of culture—hitherto a widely accepted concept in anthropology—into the study of man's social life in the highly developed world of the twentieth century. The Thomas and Znaniecki work marks a major turning point in the study of cultural differences, immigrant assimilation, and intergroup relations in the United States. The significance of this work and its methods for the present book is clear: what had previously been considered strange, deviant, and threatening behavior was now perceived as the normally expected behavior of new and strange people. Seen in its cultural context, the behavior of Polish immigrants was revealed to be as normal and as conforming as that of any American.

The criticisms of the method of using personal documents[9] really serve to clarify the perspective. Personal documents such as letters cannot be used for rigid testing, nor do they lend themselves easily to statistical manipulation. They do, however, provide basic insight into the meaning of the phenomena and, when used with the necessary qualifications, are a valuable source of data.

The method used so effectively in the study of the Polish peasant became a significant influence in the field of delinquency studies through the work of Clifford Shaw. In Chapter One of *The Jack-roller*,[10] Shaw discusses at length the value of personal documents, particularly the autobiography, for studying the causes of delinquent behavior. Strongly influenced by the work of Thomas and Znaniecki, Shaw set out to construct case histories of delinquents that would convey knowledge of the entire situation as the delinquent boy himself saw it. Shaw also sought to introduce into the case as complete a description as possible of the social and cultural background of the boy. Shaw provides an excellent model for the development of sociogenic case histories. It is helpful to recall here, however, the comment made in the Introduction of the present book: although many years ago Shaw was emphasizing the importance of cultural variables in contrast to psychological variables, he made little use of the social organizational variables, such as those emphasized in the present discussion, some of which are sought through the sociogenic case method.

Shaw began with a series of interviews with the boy. Next he gathered all available documents containing information on the boy's history (court records, histories of other delinquents who were his friends, and so on). He kept these documents mainly to use as a check on the responses of the boy himself. He then had the boy write his autobiography:

The initial step in securing the written document has been to obtain, usually by means of personal interviews, a list of the boy's behavior problems, delinquencies, arrests, court appearances and commitments. These experiences were then arranged in the order of their occurrence and presented to the boy to be used as a guide in writing "his own story." He was always instructed to give a complete and detailed description of each experience, the situation in which it occurred, and the impression it made on him. If the initial document was relatively meagre, the boy was urged to make further elaboration. The process of elaboration was continued until the story was made as complete as possible.[11]

Shaw's purpose in this technique was to obtain: (1) as complete a description as possible of the delinquent act; (2) as complete a description as possible of the cultural and social context in which the act occurred—that is, what it meant in the entire setting surrounding it; and (3) a description as to what the act meant to the boy himself. Only in this way, Shaw insisted, could a person know what the act really was: whether it represented a repudiation of law; whether it constituted a form of behavior expected of the boy in his situation; and/or whether it was the only understandable reaction to a particular difficulty. The great value of the history, as Shaw put it, was that it was the boy's own story; and the value of the investigative method was its built-in immunity to distortion or misinterpretation by the theoretical orientation of the investigator studying it. As Ernest W. Burgess comments at the end of the history presented in *The Jack-roller*, ". . . Stanley, in telling the truth as it appears to him, unwittingly reveals what we most want to know, namely, his personality reactions and his own interpretation of his experience." [12] Burgess also expressed his convictions about the importance of this kind of written history:

> First the document and others like it indicate the value for scientific purposes of materials in the first person. The boy's own story, the narratives of his parents, the verbatim family interview are objective data. Much of the material on personality now extant, including the case records of the social agencies, is vitiated for full use for research purposes by the fact that they are subjective records—that is, translations by the visitor of the language, emotional expressions and attitudes of the person interviewed. A great advance in the study of personality has been made by the development of the record in the first person. [13]

The objective of the life history, as used by Shaw, therefore, is to get at the actor's statement, as full and uninhibited as possible. On the basis of this, one may come to recognize that the boy's delinquent acts were not unusual, but followed a pattern of behavior expected among his peers. In this way, it would become clear that he was behaving according to the culture of his peers. One can then construct a statement of the actor's culture, his role prescriptions, his response to the behavior patterns into which he had been socialized, and his gradual assimilation into a "peer culture" as this had taken place. With this information, one is in a good position to perceive the meaning which the delinquent act had for the delinquent.

But the sociogenic case history method requires attention to the psychogenic variables, including unconscious motivations and organizational emphasis, of a type not supplied by Shaw.

The Organizational Emphasis

The sociogenic case study method must also seek to explain the relationship of the individual being studied to the social organizations which have structured his environment, affect his life through their power, interest, manipulation, and compromise, and provide him with his positive as well as negative reference groups and role models. A few illustrations may serve to clarify the need for an organizational emphasis in the study of social behavior.

There is little mystery about why post-Civil War Negroes were not property owners in Mississippi and why they developed patterns of social accommodation related to the survival of men without property or power. Their behavior was an adaptive response of a people to a particular historical situation. The immediate reaction of many Jews to occasional anti-Semitic statements by some Negroes during the 1968 New York City public school strike can be explained as a concern about a new manifestation of anti-Semitism; but it was also very obviously the conscious reaction of a group which saw its deeply rooted interests in the school system threatened by some of the proposals made by the more extreme segments of the Negro community.

Today, the growing militancy of younger Puerto Rican leaders in New York City toward what they perceive to be established white *and* Negro political power in the city also becomes more understandable when considered in its organizational context; it becomes even clearer when the limited number of alternative responses to such patterns of exclusion becomes evident. As C. W. M. Hart[14] pointed out, when a strike occurred in the automobile plants of Windsor, Ontario, he was not primarily interested in the direction and quality of the interaction between foreman and machinist working in the plant; he wanted to know the relationship among the Ford Motor Company, the United Automobile Workers, the Chamber of Commerce, and the Catholic Church and how all of these influenced the attitudes, perceptions, and behavior of the workers involved in the strike. These were the great organized structures which molded the lives of both employees and employers. One could understand the strike behavior of any particular striker far more clearly when he saw the individual acting in the framework of this complicated organized system. The study of these variables may be called the organizational emphasis in sociogenic case histories.

An example of this second type of emphasis applied to sociogenic case histories is found in the classic study, *The Unemployed Worker,* which E. Wight Bakke[15] did in New Haven at the Yale Institute of Human Relations during the 1930s. In the field of employment and work, this eight-year-long study did on the organizational level what the study of Thomas and Znaniecki did on the cultural level for the understanding of the immigrant. It thoroughly destroyed the conceptualization of the unemployed worker, common among employers and many of the general public at that time, as a person who drifted, was not strongly motivated, had little ability to plan, and had little concern for the future. Some of America's most recent discoveries about the life of the poor, their strengths and resources, were actually antedated by thirty years in the Bakke study. Bakke found that, when perceived within the framework of the worker's own experience and culture and within the organizational structure of the worker's own community, the unemployed man was a man of extraordinary resources, deeply held motivation, and a more impressive ability than that of his employers to cope with pressing needs. In other words, the behavior of the unemployed worker had a meaning from his point of view which was quite different from the meaning it was given when viewed from within the conceptual scheme of the employer. Bakke insisted on the importance of perceiving the experience as the worker perceived it, measured against both the cultural and organizational context of his life experience.

In the preface to his book, Bakke gives a brief description of the method used in the study:

1. Participation as unemployed men in the life and practice of the unemployed for several periods · during the eight-year interval.

2. Intensive case studies and budget investigations of twenty-five unemployed families over a period from 1932 to 1939.

3. Testing of hypotheses developed from the foregoing sources by reference to interviews with the two hundred "married and together" unemployed families appearing in a random sample of two thousand families in New Haven in 1933.

4. Investigation of a 10 per cent sample of unemployed households in New Haven in 1938 with particular interest focused on experience with unemployment compensation.

5. Interviews with social workers, ministers, public officials, and employers to check on the alleged facts disclosed in the contacts with the unemployed. Included in these was an investigation of the hiring and firing policies of a representative sample of New Haven firms.

6. Examination of numerous reports and other documentary evidence on the social and economic environment of New Haven workers and on the operation of the various social services for the benefit of the unemployed.[16]

Bakke summarized the results of his study as follows:

The picture of "the worker" we have derived from this method cannot lay claim to completeness. But it can lay claim to being the product of objective observation. What we have seen is a group of workers functioning as members of a community:

Working toward certain goals;

Within a cultural environment;

In the midst of opportunities offered and restrictions imposed by the conditions of life in the community;

With the use of their personal equipment for the task; and

By means of certain practices, economic, familial, recreational, religious, and political.

In describing the complex of realities out of which the worker comes to wrestle with the problems of unemployment, we shall use that framework. We shall portray his adjustments to unemployment as a rearrangement of that normal structure of his life and the effects of unemployment as a modification of that structure under the stress and strain of the absence of a job.[17]

Bakke's method, utilized as fully as possible, would provide in the case of a delinquent a view of delinquent behavior as it is perceived in the context of the totality of the delinquent's life situation.

The much more elaborate "Hawthorn" study,[18] which has become a classic in the field of industrial sociology, was not so much an example of a sociogenic case study as it was an example of the controlled experiment. For the purposes of this book, however, the significance of the Hawthorn study and of numerous smaller studies which followed it was their consistent discovery of the social world of the worker. While employers habitually conceptualized workers as "economic men," entirely responsive to economic motives and rewards, the dominant motivating force of the workers was their concern about maintaining their social groups, the patterns of relationship which they created and through which they found psychosocial satisfaction, recognition, prestige, protection, and a modicum of control over their own affairs. Restriction of output, particularly in the presence of premium pay for higher production, was an act which employers always condemned as uneconomical, harmful to the employee himself, and even immoral. Nevertheless, when perceived in the context of the employee's life, it appears as the means which the employee took to preserve a pattern of social relationships that were more important to him than money.

The Hawthorn study used three methods: nonparticipant

observation; intensive interviews; and controlled experiments with small groups. First, the observers set up a desk at the side of the workroom and recorded, from one end of the workday to the other, all interaction which took place between the workers. Second, they held a series of intensive interviews, sometimes using decoys such as a nurse in the company infirmary; third, they created work teams and tested their productivity in continually varying work situations.

In view of these developments in industrial sociology, it is clear that the application of the sociogenic case history method in the field of delinquency is an integral part of a wide and rich development in sociological research. In other words, it is part of the effort of investigators to reveal the meaning of the act, whether delinquent or not, in the perspective of its organizational and cultural context.

The organizational emphasis has not received the same attention as the cultural emphasis, but there may be numerous reasons for this neglect. In the first place, it is much more difficult to perceive the results of the impact of social structures on individuals than it is to perceive the influence of a culture. In the second place, organizational analysis is a relative newcomer to the field of sociology and the concepts and methods required for skillful analysis are still in short supply. Nevertheless, evidence of the skillful use of organizational analysis is available.

Two of Talcott Parsons' exercises in this method, "Age and Sex in the Social Structure of the United States," [19] and the well-known analysis of the medical profession in the classic *The Social System*,[20] are outstanding contributions to this insight. Both are based on extensive common-sense knowledge of the groups Parsons analyzes. Robert Merton's remarkable essays, "Bureaucratic Structure and Personality" [21] and "Social Structure and Anomie," [22] are also examples of the great value of this analysis when applied by a skilled person to the study of contemporary situations. One of the most extensive studies of this kind, and one of the best known, is William Whyte's *Street Corner Society*.[23] This latter provides a structural analysis on two levels: the level of the gang (the Nortons), in which the structure of the group and its influence on behavior is skillfully presented; and the level of the neighborhood, in which the political structures, business, and the rackets are described as creating an organized framework that guided behavior in particular channels, or restricted it to particular forms for greater effectiveness.

In many cases, the analysis of structural constraints in social systems, large or small, has been a matter of refining conceptual schemes and then using them for the study of one's own behavior or of that of others. For example, Chester Barnard, in *Functions of the Executive*,[24] presents an excellent analysis of the business executive as he acts within the structure of the corporation. The role of the executive is described as a position within a structure in which inevitable strains are present. He must, for instance, have information on which to base decisions, but the channels of information are often structured so that they block the information he needs. Thus he continually faces the problem of making decisions based on inadequate information. Barnard's empirical data came from his years of experience as president of a large American corporation. He was actually writing a personal case history. One could say that his scholarly contribution was the fruit of years of participant observation. In a sense, this is not unlike the method Shaw used with delinquents: as the delinquents did, the executive too reports his own personal experience; he tells his own story. But Barnard's advance over the Shaw method is the elaborate conceptual scheme, which enabled Barnard to perceive the meaning of his actions within the limiting framework of the social structure in which he was working.

The significance of this method for sociogenic case histories is that it reveals the manner in which social organizations can influence and affect an individual in terms of power and interest, for example, just as cultural norms can structure the behavior of an individual. The introduction of both cultural and organizational variables into the sociogenic case study of a delinquent reveals the content and sources of Classes 1 and 2 of

the Intervening Variables (see Figure 1) which became acti-
vated in the situations in which his delinquency occurred. They
explain more fully the youth who acts in the situation.

A review of the case material presented in this book and its
companion case volume clarifies the nexus between organizations and the behavior of the youths studied. Chapter 3 in the
present volume indicates that the neighborhood studied had recently undergone massive demographic change in a very short
time. Chapter 4 describes what happened in the area in the process of such change, particularly how the local institutions—that
is, the schools, churches, community centers, police, and so on—
were no longer as effectively meeting the needs of the residents.
Formerly these organizations were strongly and positively related to the needs of a predominantly middle-class Jewish, Italian, and Irish population. As the population shifted rapidly to
lower-class Puerto Rican and Negro, these organizations proved
incapable of keeping up with the change. They were not geared
to serving the needs of the new population in the same way they
had served the old. The result has been extensive "institutional
dislocations." [25] The school, for example, instead of helping the
youthful newcomer by adjusting to his needs, has expected him
to adjust to an institution which seldom made sense to the
youth; the life of the youth tended to become ground up in the
system. In situations like this, when the needs of youth are not
satisfied by the local institutions, when a youth gets into
"trouble," the tendency is *not* to ask, "What is wrong with the
institutions?" but, "What is wrong with the youth?" Furthermore, when the established institutions fail to relate to the lives
of youth effectively in order to meet their needs, youths begin to
create their own compensatory institutions. Thus the poolhall,
the candy store, the cellar club, even the adolescent's own apartment when his parents are absent during the day, become centers of significant action which constitute a separate world, one
noticeably alienated from the institutions and organizations of
the general community or from the world of older residents in
the neighborhood. Therefore, on the level of the institutions
which have become dislocated, or on the level of the peer group

institutions created by youths, a skillful analysis of organizational structure is essential for revealing the influences which guide the adolescent's behavior.

The Method of the Sociogenic Case History

The second part of this chapter is a presentation of the actual method of conducting a sociogenic case study—that is, of relating the cultural and organizational variables in the case to the youth himself and to his delinquent behavior. Data must first be sought about cultural background, informal social groups (peers, family, and so on), formal institutional structures (school, community center, church and so on), and the personality variables in the context of these three. These data must then be organized and analyzed in relation to data accumulated by the method of situational analysis, as presented in Chapter 2, and in terms of data obtained by the method of area analysis, as presented in Chapter 3. With this range of information systematically organized, analyzed, and interrelated, a summary assessment of the case can be drawn up. As case after case is developed in this manner for a given high-delinquency neighborhood, an in-depth understanding of the area builds up. The results of this process are illustrated in Chapter 4. Once such knowledge of an area has emerged through the combined application of the three basic methods of structural analysis over time, each succeeding case from the area must then be related to the total neighborhood gestalt into which it fits.

This procedure was followed in the series of case synopses cited for illustrative purposes throughout the present book. Full-length illustrations of this case method are presented in the companion volume, *Case Studies in the Analysis of Delinquent Behavior*. In all the cases studied, the sociogenic case history began with the delinquent action situation and worked back toward what the investigator considered the significant historical events most relevant to an understanding of the adolescent who acted in the situation. The studies begin with a *description of the complete official version of the delinquent act,* as this is available in the probation records, and the record of the boy in the training school, if he had been committed to one, and from any other established institutions with which he had come in contact. The nature and availability of court records vary with the nature of the juvenile court system in different states and the different procedures used in the correctional process. From the viewpoint of the methods explained in the present book, even the best of these records are very inadequate and likely to be misleading. They generally present psychogenic interpretations with little or no attention to cultural and organizational variables in describing the life history of the adolescent. They give an official view of the youth, a view which is generally constricted and bound by the narrow conceptual framework characteristic of the case method customarily used. Nevertheless, before anything else was done in the cases studied, as complete a case study as possible was compiled from these records.

Following this step in the procedure of the sociogenic case study, the general social and cultural identifying characteristics of the boy himself must be sought. This is always the first step in the effort to identify the general culture and subcultures to which a youth belongs, the social class and social environment in which he has been active, and the kind of family from which he has come. In order to achieve this identification, interviews must be sought with the youth himself, his peers, members of his family, and anyone who has known him well and is able to help the investigator locate the youth initially in his cultural and social setting.

After the boy has been so identified by the investigator, the case data are gathered according to the guiding interdisciplinary orientation under seven topics or headings: The Subject of the History—the Youth Himself; Peer Group Relationships; The Family; Local Institutional Ties; The Neighborhood; Cultural Variables; and Clinical Evaluation. Appropriate methods vary according to the topic being examined.

The Subject of the History—
the Youth Himself

The sociogenic case history depends critically on a relationship with the boy himself, a relationship enabling the boy to talk freely, to explain his life, his behavior, and the reasons for it, and to describe the characteristics of his neighborhood, his friends, his family, and other significant adults. There is no single effective method for getting at these data. If a boy is in custody in a training school or a detention center, he may be approached directly and with no advance notice. If he is not in custody, the ease or difficulty of approach will depend on a number of factors: whether or not the boy is willing to talk to a stranger; whether or not he is in a family situation in which he is available (mother, father, or others know where he is, will be there when he comes home, can give him messages, and so forth); whether he has a telephone or not. If a boy wishes to avoid the investigator, he can generally do so effectively. Achieving good rapport with the boy requires resourcefulness, imagination, and determination on the part of the investigator, and generally a great expenditure of time in the field. There is no way of insuring success. If a boy will not cooperate, it will probably be impossible to reach his peers. Without the cooperation of the boy and his peers, a good sociogenic case history is hardly possible.

If the adolescent is willing to talk, and most are, if approached by the right person in appropriate circumstances (which may be a poolroom at 2 A.M., or a park on a Saturday night, or the boy's home on a Sunday morning), he will give an extensive description of his past, of his understanding of the meaning of what he did, of his relationship to peers and significant adults. The report by the boy either supplements the information already on hand, or contradicts it, or gives it a meaning which it did not have before.

The data may be recorded in various ways. Sometimes circumstances do not permit the convenient use of a notebook or a tape recorder. It may be necessary to catch the youth on the fly or in a casual meeting on a street corner or in a store. In these cases, the investigator must rely on memory and write down, as soon as possible after the interview, the data he can remember. It is most important to record significant verbatim material, gestures, and other meaningful behavior. The early interviews with Pedro F., first described in the Introduction, and those with his peers were conducted this way. If the interviewer has worked out an outline of points he wishes to cover, he can generally keep the results of the interview readily in mind. The ideal method is the use of a tape recorder, but this method must be agreeable to all participants in the interview. If the tape recorder cannot be used, the taking of notes is the best substitute, provided it can be done conveniently and is agreeable to the person or persons being interviewed. Notes may be further supplemented by having the boy or his peers write out a life history.

Ordinarily, there will be a number of subsequent interviews with the youth himself. The initial interview(s) enables the investigator, with the help of his research associates, to identify the culture of the boy or the subcultures with which he may be identified. It also provides a description of the social environment in which the youth operates, as the youth himself perceives it. Most important, it provides the names and descriptions of the peers with whom he spends much of his time, as well as the general report of their activities. The peers are a vital source of information. A continuing, favorable relationship with the adolescent increases the investigator's knowledge. More specialized interviews will take place at a later point.

Peer Group Relationships

Undoubtedly the most significant influence on the youth is the peer group. Anyone who has read autobiographies such as Claude Brown's *Manchild in the Promised Land*,[26] or Piri Thomas' *Down These Mean Streets*,[27] will recognize that the world of the peer group differs greatly from every other world with which the boy is associated. Without the perspective given by the peers, it is doubtful that the history can be compiled as fully as is desirable.

The most effective and perhaps the only way to reach the peer group is through the boy himself. If he passes the word along that they may talk freely, that the investigator is to be considered a "friend," rapport with the peers is fairly easy to achieve. In the case of Pedro F., at the request of the interviewer, Pedro called his best friend, told him the interviewer was going to call and would like to talk with Pedro's friends. When the interviewer called, the friend obligingly assembled ten of Pedro's other friends and the group interview proceeded easily, yielding fruitful results. The interviews with the peers may be with individuals or groups. It is particularly helpful to do the interviews both ways, to meet the peers in group situations, when the interaction between them can be observed, and also individually, when they can more freely express some of their personal convictions to the interviewer.

The authors have found that the peer group is the most valuable source of information about a youth, his neighborhood, and the activities of his group. Not only can the peer group place the act of the boy in a context which helps clarify its meaning for the boy, but it also corrects the limitations or personal biases or lack of information characteristic of the boy himself. The observations of the peers stem from intimate familiarity, yet they have an objective viewpoint about what kind of a boy their friend is, how he behaves in normal, ordinary circumstances in the neighborhood where he lives, what they think of the way he acts. In this framework the investigator can more reliably assess whether the actions of the boy were considered "normal" by others in the circumstances in which they occurred. For example, if the boy lives in a neighborhood marked by violence, and if he is violent, what does his violence mean, as perceived by the peer group? Is violence *per se* normal? Are certain kinds of violence abnormal? If the boy was stealing, is theft a cultural pattern among his peers? Thus the meaning of the boy's act begins to emerge through the meaning it had for the significant others among his peers.

In the case studies presented in the companion volume, it will be evident that one of the most difficult tasks of the research staff was establishing contact with the peer group. This was done most effectively in the case of Pedro F. It was much more difficult in other cases, either because the subject of the case study was reluctant to make the necessary introductions or because his peers could not be reached easily. However, in the study of youths from the Bronx neighborhood described in the chapters ahead, the research staff perceived that the paths of the youths under study crossed each other. Interviews with a number of local adolescents revealed a general pattern of youth activity in the neighborhood. As a result, the characteristics of peer group life in the neighborhood, and its influence on the behavior of the youths under study, became very clear. Poolrooms, coffee shops, and store hangouts were pinpointed; attitudinal patterns toward school and truancy became evident; the widespread use and sale of marijuana, as well as adolescent conflict between nearby long-resident Italian youths and Negro and Puerto Rican newcomers, were seen as significant features of peer group life. Some of the staff members were able to associate with the youths at some of their hangouts and observe at close range the style of activity which took place.

The Family

A great deal of information about the family is presented in the available official records. It is probably the most extensively studied context of the offender's life in the routine preparation of cases. However, the kinds of data required for an understanding of the cultural background of the boy and his family are generally missing. It is not sufficient to know that children of three different fathers are present in the home or that the father and mother have never been married; for this information will usually be interpreted according to the norms of the dominant American culture, and the interpretation can be very unfavorable to the boy and his parents. Rather it is necessary to know what these situations mean in the culture from which the family has come and in which it interacts. Extramarital sexual relations in the culture of poor Negro families are viewed very differently by the Negro families involved than by middle-class observers, white or Negro. Therefore the study of the family, according to the sociogenic case method, is designed to reveal the cultural background of the family and, consequently, the meaning of the boy's behavior in terms of that cultural background.

The data from the official records combined with initial interviews with the family should enable the interviewer or others to identify the general culture of the family and to determine, for example, whether it is a migrant, rural, southern Negro family or a family with long experience in a northern slum; whether it is from a town in Puerto Rico where consensual unions are rare or from a town where they are common; whether the family is from an area where people have a reputation for toughness or from a section where people are known to be mild-mannered. The official case record of Pedro F., for example, indicated that his people had come from Fajardo, a town which has had a high rate of consensual unions and whose people have acquired the nickname in Puerto Rico of *Caraduros,* meaning "hard-faced" or "hard-headed ones." In addition, a study of the social variables should enable the investigator to identify the family as lower middle class, or lower class, as the case may be. Once this is done for apprehended delinquents, who are usually lower class, the investigator can proceed to identify the style of life which is characteristic of the particular family being studied.

In the case studies presented in the companion volume, attempts have been made to identify the families of each of the youths according to five different life styles among American urban, lower-class populations: *strivers, consistent copers, inconsistent copers, relievers,* and *hold-overs.*[28] The use of these concepts does not imply an effort to rate these families according to their "worth." It merely ranks them according to their relative compatibility with the core culture of industrialized, urbanized, and highly competitive America. The differential value orientations in each of the family types equip the participants differently for participation in the urban middle class. Thus strivers are more employable or already employed, are more anxious to move upward when given the opportunity, and are more likely to have children who are doing well in school and who are also apt to be only slightly involved in delinquent behavior. At the other end of the scale, the variables of employability and delinquency appear to reverse themselves progressively and drastically in the case of the hold-overs. Hold-overs who linger on in urban slums, sharing the maladapted life of alcoholics, derelicts, psychotics, addicts, and the "hard-core families" at the bottom of the heap, are almost totally unemployable, while at the same time highly delinquent in a chaotic, disorganized way. In the middle of the hierarchy, where the inconsistent copers stand, employability is mixed, with work being intermittent and often at jobs on the docks or in construction, where work may be casual and a daily "shape-up" customary. Delinquency rates in this group tend to be very high and often of the violent gang type. The key to understanding inconsistent copers is that they have a life style which emphasizes fun, excitement, thrills, and a general escape from boredom and routine. It is rare that a family fits perfectly into any category, but a reasonable identification can usually be made. Once made, it provides a helpful perspective with which to assess the behavior of family members. From a similar point of view, the Committee on the Family, Group for the Advancement of Psychiatry at Harvard University,[29] is engaged in extensive cross-cultural study in an effort to clarify, in terms meaningful for psychiatric diagnosis, what a family is. They have also pointed out the danger of using the American middle-class model in identifying family relationships. The cultural role in the Puerto Rican family, for example, of the grandparent, the *compadre,* the relative, or the friend must be kept in mind. The absence of a father may not imply the absence of significant male figures in a boy's life. In this way, a knowledge of the culture, of the social class, particularly of the subcultures of the lower class, enables the investigator to describe the family and its relationship to the delinquent more adequately.

It is important to understand how the family judges the behavior of the youth. Is it considered deviant? If so, deviant from what, and how seriously deviant? The objective of the interviewer is to learn the "normal" situation and how the acts defined as delinquent are related to what is considered normal by the family involved and the subculture it shares. Charles Hughes makes the point clearly in an excellent discussion of the life history:

> Insofar as what we call "sick," is sick only by reference to some standards of health, we can use biographical materials to help obtain understanding of the nature of nonpathology. . . . What is the developmental study of the personality in its natural habitat, its confrontation with goals and new complexes of expectations as it proceeds through life, its strategies for problem solving, adjustments and adaptation, its mechanisms for maintaining equilibrium? [30]

Identifying the culture and subcultures of the family and of the boy is not something done once and then set aside as complete. Awareness and insight into the cultural variables continue to increase as familiarity with the family and its cultural identifications and organizational location within the broader community grows.

Ease of approach to families differs widely. Some families studied for this book were very responsive to interviews by the research staff. Generally these were families which saw the investigator as a person who might be of assistance to their boy in trouble. Other families were difficult, if not impossible, to approach. In one of the cases studied but not reported in the companion case volume, the research staff, including the psychiatrist, tried a half-dozen times to interview the family, especially the mother and the youth's older sister. All such efforts were made by visits to their apartment. Still all attempts were to no avail. The sister was never seen by the staff, and the mother artfully and politely dodged each interview situation. On the other hand, in the case of Henry R., described earlier in this chapter, the family was most cooperative and courteous in speaking with the staff members and in helping them to maintain contact with Henry.

Approaches to families can be made through the youth, through his probation officer, through a social agency which has been in contact with him, or through some effective social contact such as a clergyman or schoolteacher. In their work on cases from the neighborhood described in Chapter 3, the staff initially approached the families directly without introduction. It was later decided, however, that, since all the cases studied were on probation, a much more effective approach could be made to each of them through the probation officer who knew them. As a result, data on families are uneven. As is evident from the case studies in the companion volume, in some a very reliable identification of family culture and subculture can be made; in others, not.

Local Institutional Ties

The increasing knowledge the investigator has of the youth, his peers, and his family, together with data from the official record, will provide understanding of the institutions of the local area which have touched the boy's life. These include schools, churches, police, community centers, clubs, and so forth. In applying the interdisciplinary methodology to the study of delinquency in a given area, an extensive knowledge of local institutions will already be available to an investigator doing a study of a particular case from that area. The specific objective of examining local institutions through the sociogenic case history method is to study the relationship of the youth being examined to the local institutions and of the institutions to the youth. A secondary objective is to provide additional information about local institutions as seen by local residents.

Interviews with knowledgeable persons associated with the local institutions will provide clues to the attitudes various institutions hold with respect to the youth being studied. Interviews with the youth himself, his peers, his family, and others who are identified with him will enable the investigator to know what the youth and his friends think about the local institutions. It is of vital importance here to understand how the youth himself relates to these institutions: Does he see them as helpful, threatening, meaningless? Why does he think this way? Do the peer group and family agree with the youth's opinion? Why do the institutions view him as they do? Through answers to questions such as these, the institutional structure of a neighborhood, particularly in its impact on the life and behavior of a local adolescent, becomes clearer.

The Neighborhood

The sociogenic case study will already have uncovered a great deal of data about the neighborhood or milieu in which the youth lived. An intensive effort must be made, however, to amplify this knowledge. Understanding the area enables the investigator to identify major environmental variables related to the delinquent act. For example, in preparing case studies, staff members active in the area were also continually engaged in a study of neighborhood variables.

These variables must be examined from three different dimensions. First, at the moment of the delinquent act, they usually constitute a key element in the situation and, as such, are studied as part of situational analysis, a method described in the following chapter. Second, they are studied as part of the method of area analysis illustrated in Chapter 3. The data employed in area analysis will indicate significant features of the neighborhood, such as extremely rapid population change, poor housing, overcrowded schools, gross unemployment, unusual population distributions, invasion, or flight. Finally, the neighborhood variables are an important element in the sociogenic case study itself.

The particular aspects of the neighborhood variables to which the sociogenic case study addresses itself are the actor's reaction to his neighborhood and the influence of the neighborhood on the development of the youth. This knowledge of the neighborhood complements the description provided by the method of area analysis and, as case study is added to case study, adds progressively to the information available about the neighborhood.

In preparing a single case, many others besides the youth, his peers, and his family are interviewed. These include knowledgeable local informants, such as merchants, storekeepers, local youth workers, clergymen, political leaders, school principals, settlement house personnel, and, finally, the police, whose knowledge of the area is unique and extremely valuable. The interviews are further supplemented by visits to the area, direct observation, exploratory walks at various times of the day or night, or actual work in the area by community organizers. The purpose of this kind of inquiry in relation to the sociogenic case history is to gain a "feel" for the area, in addition to concrete information about it, for a better understanding of the organizational and cultural context of the youth's life and activity and also in order to view his development as a person in the framework of his environment.

Thus it is important to know historical details such as answers to the following: Had this been a quiet middle-class area until a large low-income housing project was suddenly built in its midst? Were poor people relocated to this section from an urban redevelopment area? Did the sudden influx of Negroes and Puerto Ricans or others lead to a change in the centers of political power? Were the newcomers greeted with hostility? Did the arrival of new residents lead to a loss of jobs by older residents? For example, did the Italians replace the Irish as longshoremen? Or did Puerto Ricans replace Negroes as apartment house "supers" and other custodial employees? What happened to the schools when the neighborhood population shifted radically? This is the kind of historical reference against which organizational and cultural variables in given cases should be reflected, thus clarifying the meaning of the delinquent acts under examination.

Cultural Variables

With the above data assembled and organized, a full analysis of the cultural variables is made possible. As indicated above, a number of cultural levels will be involved. For example, if the adolescent is a Puerto Rican boy, it is obvious that he will share a number of general cultural patterns characteristic of Puerto Ricans. He will also be a member of a subculture. He may be from a mountain village or from a settlement of sugar cane workers on the coast; he may come from the urban working class or from an urban slum. Finally, he may belong to one or more smaller subcultures, such as that of a primary group of peers, a particular kind of family, or some other reference group. Once the delinquent can be sufficiently identified according to these variables, the investigator can begin to determine which characteristics of the youth's behavior reflect features of the culture or subculture of which he is a member.

The analysis of behavior in the context of culture seeks to identify the behavior patterns which are expected or required by people who share the way of life of a particular culture. It also seeks to clarify the values which underlie the behavior patterns, the meaning which the behavior has for the people of the culture under study. The behavior patterns commonly fall into two classes: *folkways,* consisting of patterns of expected behavior in which the value content is relatively minor, such as modes of dress, manners of greeting, modes of eating, and so forth; and *mores,* consisting of patterns of behavior in which the value content is relatively serious, or socially shared definitions of rules which are considered crucial, even sacred, such as the practice of monogamy in contrast to polygamy, free selection of a marriage partner in contrast to having a partner selected by one's parents, women's right to an education equal to that of men; and so forth.

An example of folkways is found in the case of Miguel S., a case studied but not reported in the companion case volume. This Puerto Rican youth faced a conflict within his own family about the interpretation of his behavior. Miguel, at age fifteen, was the eldest male in his household; he, therefore, saw no reason to explain his late hours to his mother, sisters, or brothers. The family, however, still viewed him as a boy who should be subservient and respectful and who should explain his late hours to his mother. She brought him to Family Court on a complaint of incorrigibility. Interestingly, Miguel never criticized his mother for her action. He implied that she actually agreed with his own definition of his behavior but had been pressured by other people to take him to court.

An example of mores is found in the case of Henry R., cited earlier. It was clear that premarital sexual relations at an early age were not viewed as deviant by the particular Negro community to which Henry belonged.

Details of the culture and subcultures involved in a particular sociogenic case history are gathered by interviews with the youth who is the subject of the study, with his family or peer group, and with knowledgeable outsiders. The youth's family may then be identified according to its particular subcultural affiliation. One also looks for indications of group expectations among the adolescent's peers. These constitute another subculture, in a way similar to that of unemployed workers whom Bakke studied in New Haven or among the workers in the bank wiring room described by Roethlisberger and Dickson. In the study of these adolescent subcultures,[31] it is necessary to determine the patterns of expected behavior of the group, the extent to which the youth under study conforms to these patterns, and the judgments made about his behavior by other members of his subculture. Was it behavior they would expect or enforce, even though it was defined as delinquent by outsiders? Did participants in the subculture also consider the behavior a deviation from their norms?

Clinical Evaluation

The examination of all the variables described above now makes it possible to examine all the Intervening Variables relating to the characteristics of the youth's personality. The primary focus at this point will be on Class 3 of the Intervening Variables as described in Figure 1. Examination of these in the cases studied is the function of the psychiatrist, working with other members of the research staff. In conducting his personality evaluation, the psychiatrist takes advantage of the abundant data available about the social and cultural context in which the adolescent he is examining had been acting.

In carrying out his role, the clinician needs to determine: (1) if any psychopathology exists in the delinquent; (2) if it does exist, whether it is related to the delinquent activity; and (3) if it is related, how it is related.

A clinical examination in depth, focusing on the internal dynamics present, should reveal the state of ego (personality) organization and functioning, on the basis of the amount and degree of anxiety present, the defense mechanisms used to cope with unconscious conflicts, distortions of reality, and the youth's ability or inability to deal with life situations in his *particular* world.

Although such a clinical examination may not determine the contributing etiological factors, it should allow the examiner to ascertain the presence or absence of psychopathology. To determine more accurately the degree of psychopathology and the causative factors involved, as well as the relative importance of different contributing factors, the psychiatrist should understand the cultural and organizational elements relevant to the life and development of the individual. These elements have been made available to him, prior to the examination, by sociogenic case methods. The more familiar the psychiatrist is with these factors, the better able will he be to evaluate properly their relative importance, as compared with the unique intrapsychic phenomena and interpersonal experiences of the individual, in contributing to his behavior and personality structure. It should be expected that, whatever the psychiatrist's personal familiarity with the various cultural and organizational influences may be, he will have to make use of the social scientist's knowledge, which in this area will be broader and more intensive than his own.

This information will help shed light on the remaining aspects of the problem—the determination of whether the psychopathology, if present, is related to the boy's *behavior* (in this case, his delinquent activity) and, if so, how it is related. Study of delinquency from the structural standpoint as described in the various other parts of this book yields good information in all environmental areas and much about the social psychological aspects of the delinquent's personality as described by Classes 1 and 2 of the Intervening Variables in Figure 1. But these data fail to contribute significantly to an understanding of the unconscious meaning of the delinquent act to the youth who commits it. The knowledge of cultural and organizational influences may offer clues to the unconscious meaning of delinquency, which may be expressive of the individual's psychopathology or which may turn out to be entirely unrelated to it.

For example, in the case of Henry R., cited earlier in this chapter, clinical examination found the boy to be schizophrenic. But the psychiatrist could find no evidence of a relationship between the personality disorder of the youth and the youth's behavior, which was defined by the court as delinquent. Had the youth suffered from no personality disorder at all, the sociogenic case study indicates that he would almost certainly have been involved in the same delinquency (early sexual experiences), which was in fact a common pattern of behavior for his family and peers.

The psychiatrist's examination should also include data of a biologic nature, as called for by one set of Independent Variables in Figure 1, so that, in the evaluation of the collated information, traits such as impulsivity, hyperactivity, and other possibly constitutional or genetic factors are not overlooked.

A brief mention of the role of psychological testing is necessary at this point. Some projective tests, or parts thereof, as well as a very limited number of intelligence tests, are considered relatively culture-free or cross-cultural in nature. However, the majority of projective and intelligence tests are not.[32] For these, it is necessary for the psychologist, as well as for the psychiatrist, to take into full consideration all aspects of the socially and culturally relevant forces affecting the subject in order to give his most informed opinion as to whether psychopathology or restricted intelligence is present and, if so, whether and in what way it may be related to his delinquent activity.

When all the data required by a sociogenic case history are at hand, and when these have been combined with those revealed by situational analysis and the method of area analysis, the opportunity will be present to assess the meaning the delinquency had for the youth involved, in the full context within which it occurred. At this point, too, contrasts between this level of meaning and the meaning assigned to the behavior by parents, other local adults, and authorities, as described in the next chapter on situational analysis, may also be developed.

As knowledge about different youths involved with authorities in a given area or neighborhood accumulates through individual sociogenic case histories, knowledge about the neighborhood itself, in terms of the structural supports it provides for delinquency, can also be expected to increase. As described in Chapter 4, when this understanding is combined with demographic and other data about the neighborhood, there emerges a much fuller knowledge of the area and the patterns of delinquency occurring in it.

As the data for each sociogenic case study are gathered, and assessments drawn, a full report is written for each case. In this final analytic process, the data from situational and area analysis are brought together to prepare each single sociogenic case history. Three studies of youths done in this manner are presented in the companion volume on case studies.

References

1. John M. Martin and Joseph P. Fitzpatrick, *Delinquent Behavior: A Redefinition of the Problem.* New York: Random House, 1965, p. 164.
2. *Ibid.,* p. 166 ff.
3. Socialization is here defined as the process of communicating the culture to the biological human infant so that he under-

stands it and uses it in his behavior, or as the process of communicating a subculture to those not already familiar with it. See Arnold M. Rose, *Sociology: The Study of Human Relations*. New York: Knopf, 1956, p. 567.

4. See Martin and Fitzpatrick, *op. cit.*, pp. 63–71, for a discussion of these theories.

5. Julian B. Rotter, *Clinical Psychology*. Englewood Cliffs, N.J.: Prentice-Hall, 1964, pp. 57–58.

6. Philip Klein, "Social Casework," in Edwin R. Seligman and Alvin Johnson, eds., *Encyclopedia of the Social Sciences*. New York: Macmillan, 1937, V, 177.

7. See, for example, the contrast in the lives of an Irish boy and a Puerto Rican boy who grew up two blocks apart from each other on the West Side of New York, as presented in Charlotte L. Mayerson, *Two Blocks Apart*. New York: Holt, Rinehart and Winston, 1965. The meaning of school and all associated with it is very different for Peter Quinn than it is for Juan Gonzales. Quitting school for Peter would have been a serious deviation from traditional family practice; for Juan, it would have been conformity to family practice.

8. W. I. Thomas and Florian Znaniecki, *The Polish Peasant in Europe and America*, 2 vols. New York: Dover Publications, 1958. This work was originally published in 1918.

9. Herbert Blumer, *Critique of Research in the Social Sciences: I. An Appraisal of Thomas and Znaniecki's "The Polish Peasant in Europe and America."* New York: Social Science Research Council, 1939; also Louis Gottschalk, Clyde Kluckhohn, and Robert Angell, *The Use of Personal Documents in History, Anthropology and Sociology*, Bulletin 53. New York: Social Science Research Council, 1947.

10. Clifford R. Shaw, *The Jack-roller*. Chicago: University of Chicago Press, 1930. Copyright 1930, by the University of Chicago Press. Reprinted by permission of the publisher.

11. *Ibid.*, p. 22.

12. *Ibid.*, p. 188.

13. *Ibid.*, p. 187.

14. C. W. M. Hart, "Industrial Relations Research and Social

Theory," *The Canadian Journal of Economics and Political Science* 15:53–74 (February 1949).

15. E. Wight Bakke, *The Unemployed Worker*. New Haven: Yale University Press, 1940. Reprinted by permission of the publisher.

16. *Ibid.*, p. x.

17. *Ibid.*, p. xiii.

18. Fritz J. Roethlisberger and William J. Dickson, *Management and the Worker*. Cambridge, Mass.: Harvard University Press, 1947.

19. Talcott Parsons, "Age and Sex in the Social Structure of the United States," *American Sociological Review* 7:604–616 (October 1942).

20. Talcott Parsons, *The Social System*. New York: Free Press, 1951, Chap. 10.

21. Robert K. Merton, *Social Theory and Social Structure*, rev. and enl. ed. New York: Free Press, 1957, Chap. 6.

22. *Ibid.*, Chap. 4.

23. William F. Whyte, *Street Corner Society*. Chicago: University of Chicago Press, 1943.

24. Chester Barnard, *Functions of the Executive*. Cambridge, Mass.: Harvard University Press, 1938.

25. For a more general discussion of this concept, see Peter Marris and Martin Rein, *Dilemmas of Social Reform: Poverty and Community Action in the United States*. New York: Atherton Press, 1967, Chap. 2.

26. Claude Brown, *Manchild in the Promised Land*. New York: Macmillan, 1965.

27. Piri Thomas, *Down These Mean Streets*. New York: Knopf, 1967.

28. Madeline H. Engel, "A Reconsideration of the Concept 'American Lower Class': A Study of Urban Subcultures," unpublished doctoral dissertation, Department of Sociology and Anthropology, Fordham University, 1966.

29. The Committee on the Family, Group for the Advancement of Psychiatry, *The Family Case History*. Cambridge, Mass.: Harvard University, Department of Social Relations, unpublished Working Paper, 1966.

30. Charles C. Hughes, "Life History in Cross-Cultural Research," in Jane Murphy and Alexander Leighton, eds., *Approaches to Cross-Cultural Psychiatry*. Ithaca, N.Y.: Cornell University Press, 1965, p. 290. A good example of the relativity of social definitions of mental disturbance is found in Lloyd H. Rogler and August B. Hollingshead, "The Puerto Rican Spiritualist as Psychiatrist," *American Journal of Sociology* 67:17–21 (January 1961). If a poor Puerto Rican suffering from behavior disorders goes to a psychiatrist or a mental hospital, he is defined by his community as "crazy" and is ostracized. If he goes to a spiritualist, his difficulty is defined as the result of evil spirits. His community considers this to be a "normal" spiritual experience and treats him with understanding and sympathy. Rogler and Hollingshead, by the way, were both impressed by the ability of the spiritualist to keep a mentally disturbed person functional in his community.

31. Delinquent subcultures are well described in the literature. For three good statements, see Albert K. Cohen, *Delinquent Boys: The Culture of the Gang*. New York: Free Press, 1955; Richard A. Cloward and Lloyd E. Ohlin, *Delinquency and Opportunity*. New York: Free Press, 1960; and Lewis Yablonsky, *The Violent Gang*. New York: Macmillan, 1962.

32. See, e.g., Frank Riessman and S. M. Miller, "Social Class and Projective Tests," in Frank Riessman, Jerome Cohen, and Arthur Pearl, eds., *Mental Health of the Poor*. New York: Free Press, 1964, pp. 248–258.

Chapter 2

THE SITUATIONAL
ANALYSIS OF
DELINQUENT BEHAVIOR

The Theory of Situational Analysis

Situational analysis assumes that human behavior occurs in social situations and is a consequence of the fields of forces operating in those situations. These forces include patterns of expectation brought to bear on a given situation by its participants as well as the physical aspects of that situation. Situational analysis also involves the meaning assigned to given situations by outsiders, who render judgments or evaluations of such situations and their participants. In the study of deviant behavior, "outsiders" are those who both make and enforce the rules which deviants violate.[1]

In recent years this general view has found expression in psychology, psychiatry, and sociology. The situational approach is seen in the work of the field theorists in psychology, exemplified by the experiments of Kurt Lewin and his associates. Lewin persistently emphasized that, to understand human behavior, the investigator must always consider "the relation of the concrete individual to the concrete situation." [2]

Lewin set himself in opposition to those who view human behavior as reducible to the characteristics of individuals exhibiting certain biological or psychological traits analyzed simply in terms of their historical antecedents. Among others following in the Lewinian tradition are David Krech and Richard Crutchfield,[3] Theodore Newcomb and others,[4] Leon Festinger,[5] Richard Sears,[6] and Harry Stack Sullivan.[7]

The concept of the situation entered sociological literature through the work of W. I. Thomas and Florian Znaniecki, who, in *The Polish Peasant*,[8] emphasized the importance of determining the actor's "definition of the situation." The authors demonstrated how situational definitions are transmitted from generation to generation to form distinct subcultural points of view. Talcott Parsons more recently used the term "orientation" to describe how different ways of perceiving can be explained by understanding how actors are variously oriented to the different parts of the social system.[9]

Contemporary role theory has also contributed to understanding behavior in its situational context. In regard to this, Leonard Cottrell said: "Dealing with human behavior in terms of roles requires that any item of behavior must always be placed in some self-other context." [10] Theodore Sarbin points out that role-role and self-role conflict follow from ambiguous role expectations.[11] Role-role conflict, for example, results from two conflicting expectations of behavior in the situation. An illustration would be the conflict between teacher-student expectations and peer group expectations when the student is confronted by a teacher in the presence of his peer group. The teacher expects the student to be submissive; at the same time his peers expect him to be dominant.

Thus, analysis of situational fields is based upon the theory that regardless of whether the investigator approaches human events from the standpoint of the modification of individual attitudes or from that of altering situational patterns, the initial focus is on the direct analysis of situations. Embedded in concrete situations, the attitudes of interacting individuals may be seen working against and within the framework of institutional patterns and group norms. The structural analysis of social behavior thus involves a long and hard look at the situations in which such behavior occurs. An attempt must be made to analyze these situations by looking at events which occur within them through the eyes of the participants. The most adequate understanding of the components at work in situations results from the reconstruction of what happened and why, as viewed by each participant. Operating on the situational model, the investigator moves first into the immediate "actor-in-the-situation" dimension to absorb all relevant vantage points. He seeks to learn how the actor (ego) perceives the situation in which he is acting and to learn how the other participants (alters) in the situation perceive it. Implicit within this model is the assumption that *no participant perceives the totality of any situation*. Each participant sees the part that is relevant to him, and this part is determined primarily by the participant's internalization of the expectations of others with whom he is interacting in terms of his contemporary social experiences and with whom he has previously interacted during his relevant earlier social development.

This method, applied to the study of delinquent acts, does not seek to describe the totality of a delinquent's past social history. The specific concern is to describe self-other expectations as experienced by the delinquent at the time they structured for him his perceptions of means-ends relations in the immediate situation within which his delinquent behavior occurred. In the study of given delinquent acts, the case historian, as described in the previous chapter, must assemble all relevant self-other expectations which the delinquent brings to the particular action situation. The situational analyst must determine the situational configurations as perceived by the delinquent and also as perceived by others who are directly involved in the situation or who later make judgments about it. It is also the goal of the situational analyst to describe the concrete situation within which a particular delinquent act occurred so that all relevant aspects of that situation are clearly stated.

Included as components of the delinquent action situation

are: (1) the specific delinquent act or series of acts; (2) the relationships existing between the various participants; (3) the relevant physical and structural dimensions of the situation, such as its ecological or territorial setting, as well as its specific physical setting—street corner or poolroom; and (4) the patterns of expectations involved in defining the situation by both participants and "outsiders."

As specified in the Introduction, three major networks of social expectations would appear to be generally applicable in the situational analysis of the delinquent behavior of most juveniles appearing before or otherwise being dealt with by official agencies:

—the *dominant cultural expectations* of schoolteachers, police officers, judges, probation officers, psychiatrists, and other "outsiders" who make judgments about the delinquent and his behavior;

—the *lower-class and minority-group subcultural expectations* of the delinquent held by parents and other adults who come from the same local communities as the delinquent himself;*

—the *peer group subcultural expectations* of the delinquent and of his adolescent friends and acquaintances.

All three are cultural in nature. Yet their content is very likely to be different and often in conflict. In Howard Becker's terms, dominant expectations are those held by "rule creators" and "rule enforcers," while the other two kinds of expectations are those often held by "rule breakers." [12] This is so, in the case of official delinquency at least, since rule creators and enforcers are usually middle class and very often white, while rule break-

---

* It would seem that situational analysis might also be applied with profit to acts of delinquency committed by adolescents who are, or at least appear to be, middle class. Significant subcultural differences emerged, for example, when situational analysis was applied to the delinquent behavior of Bill C., a middle-class youth discussed later in this chapter. In this case, minority-group expectations were not involved, yet social class variations and peer group expectations remained pivotal.

ers are usually lower class and are often nonwhite; age differences are also involved in that juvenile delinquent rule breakers are by definition children or adolescents, while those who create and enforce the rules they break are adults. Even when rule creators and enforcers are from the same social class and ethnic groups as are delinquent rule breakers, the age difference is present.

Situational analysis begins with the delinquent action situation (abbreviated "act-sit") to be examined. The analysis starts at a particular point in time and space. The time is the moment at which the act-sit took place; the space is the specific setting in which the act-sit unfolded as this setting is itself encompassed within a larger neighborhood. In turn, this neighborhood is itself ecologically related to a wider community.

In developing the sociogenic life history of the delinquent actor in the action situation, according to the method outlined in the previous chapter, the case historian moves back to *past* act-sit experiences of the actor to determine the relevant aspects of his life history which affected his behavior in the *present* act-sit. In this manner, past act-sit experiences of the delinquent being studied shed light upon the predispositions which he brought with him, as it were, to the present act-sit within which his delinquency occurred. In terms of the interdisciplinary scheme (Figure 1) described in the previous chapter, these predispositions are the Intervening Variables which guide and structure the actor's delinquent behavior in the act-sit being examined.

Area analysis, as illustrated in the following chapter, provides some general information about the neighborhood in which the act-sit occurred and about the ecological relationships between the area and the wider community. This information describes some of the characteristics of the more general field within which the act-sit took place, whereas the method of situational analysis describes the specific setting in which the delinquent action situation—such as school hallway, street corner, or coffee shop—unfolded. Data about the three different, often conflicting, social expectations—*dominant cultural, lower-class*

and minority-group subcultural, and *peer group subcultural*—
brought to bear on the delinquent actor and his behavior in the
act-sit under study are also provided by the method of situational analysis. These data are central to the method of situational analysis of delinquent behavior. In developing them, the
investigator "moves vertically," so to speak, in his analysis, proceeding from one level of social expectation to the next as he
looks for agreement or disagreement between the varying descriptions of the delinquent, his behavior, and why the action
occurred—the descriptions being provided by informants at all
three levels.

The nature and degree of divergence among these three
networks of social expectation converging on the delinquent act-
sit are of primary interest. An adolescent principally oriented to
middle-class values and norms has incorporated dominant cultural expectations. His delinquency, in terms of its social psychological sources, may be quite different from the delinquency
of the boy primarily oriented to lower-class and minority-group,
or to peer group, subcultural expectations. Thus the same delinquent act may have quite different meanings for each delinquent
involved, depending upon which of the three levels of expectations is primary in his orientation at the time he commits it.

In determining the patterns of expectations involved in the
situation in which a given delinquent act occurred, primary attention is given to relating the expectations of the delinquent to
his reference-membership groups[13] operative in the situation. It
is assumed that the most influential expectations, insofar as the
delinquent is concerned, derive from the norms of his reference
groups. Members of these groups may be either physically present in the situation or merely symbolically "present" through the
internal role they play in the delinquent's mind.

A main goal of the sociogenic life history is to trace the
development of individual reference group needs back through
relevant lines of the individual's social experience. With the data
provided by the life history, the investigator can identify the in-
ternalized reference group set of the individual delinquent being
examined. These are the social components of the Intervening

Variables (see Figure 1, Chapter 1) which characterize the delinquent actor and which are important influences predisposing him to react in given ways in given situations. As Newcomb points out, ". . . people differ in what they bring to the situation, and hence, within limits set by the situation, in how they respond to it." [14] To determine the full range of Intervening Variables, both socially induced as well as strictly idiosyncratic, which the delinquent brought to the delinquent act-sit being examined requires data about the delinquent's personality development in its social, psychological, and psychiatric dimensions. The principal source of data bearing on these variables is the individual delinquent himself or those closely identified with him, as elicited through interviews.

The central task is to determine the meaning of the delinquent act for the delinquent. To do this, it is necessary first to place the act in the context of the delinquent's reference groups and his subcultural identifications. Against this background the investigator seeks to work out the private meaning of the act to the delinquent. To the extent that the delinquent is able to report freely and spontaneously his feelings regarding the act-sit, psychiatric examination can make a determination of the presence or absence of unconscious distortions of meaning. For example, possession of a weapon may mean: (1) protection against a real threat in the concrete life situation of the delinquent; or (2) primarily an unconscious defensive reaction against a threatening experience looming out of the individual's past; or (3) it may involve both meanings. Any given delinquent act may or *may not* have a private unconscious meaning to the delinquent involved. One of the tasks in situational analysis is to determine the likelihood of the presence or absence of such meaning. To accomplish this the investigator must assess the social meaning the act has at the peer group level. The situational analyst is also interested in the social meanings assigned to the act at the lower-class and minority-group level of expectations, and at the dominant level of expectations as well, and in developing the contrasts in meaning among the three levels.

Also relevant to situational analysis are the stimuli pro-

vided by the physical and other structural aspects of the immediate setting itself and by the geographic area of its location.
Some of the structural components involved are: territorial
boundaries which separate the activities of different groups competing for rights in various local geographic areas; the presence
of minority communities; the density of the adolescent population per adult population; and the "strength" and the "weakness" of various sets of social definitions operating in the local
area. These and other "external" components of the situation set
conditions within which the goal-oriented behavior of the delinquent in the situation must be worked out.

These objective conditions are important, but the crucial
variable is the delinquent's own perception of the act-sit. This
variable determines his selection of means to achieve his ends.
Even the ends themselves are specified for the delinquent by his
particular perceptual scheme. In explaining a given delinquent
act, the task of the sociogenic case history method is to supply
the relevant social and cultural variables which have been at
work in the development of the Intervening Variables characteristic of the delinquent. The purpose of area analysis is to provide
an overview of the field or set of external conditions within
which the delinquent operates and has operated.[15] The task of
situational analysis is to describe the immediate act-sit in which
the delinquency occurred and to then give it meaning by describing it in terms of its setting and the three levels of social expectations, as noted above. Finally, the task is to contrast the meaning developed in the data at these three levels and to assign some
priority of interpretation to what the delinquent did and why he
did it.

Methodological Implications of Situational Analysis

Methods of research are determined by the type of problem
to be investigated. *The central thesis of this chapter is that social
behavior cannot be understood apart from the situation in which*

it occurs. It follows that delinquent behavior can only be understood by a careful and detailed examination of the actor functioning in the situation in which his delinquency occurred. The most significant implication of this statement of the problem from the standpoint of methodology lies in the necessity to re-create the delinquent act in the situation of its enactment. To do this, it is essential to obtain data that will enable the observer to re-create as much of the total situation as possible.

Situational analysis of the delinquent act begins with a description of the action situation in the "language of everyday life," since this is the language of the participants and it is to them that the investigator first turns for data. Efforts to place the actor in the act-sit must not cause the investigator to overlook the fact that each individual reacts selectively to the norms of the dominant culture, to the particular norms of his social class and ethnic subcultures, and to those of his own peers.

Llewellyn Queener indicates that in order to understand and predict one person's response to another it is necessary to know not only that he is human, but also that he is of a given culture, class, caste, and sex, and perhaps also to know him in a given crisis and in a given group and in terms of certain personal characteristics derived from his own particular social history. Queener further points out that "To forget any one of these variables, is to let it vary without our knowledge, is to lower our understanding . . ." [16]

In situational analysis, the investigator must include a method for obtaining data on how the delinquent perceives and interprets the situation, and thus, on how he imposes upon it his own socially derived norms. In keeping with Queener's point, the method must also gather data about social status characteristics of the various participants in the situation and about the crisis or incident upon which the situation centers. In addition, the method requires data about the setting itself and about the participants as seen from the standpoint of outsiders, whose expectations may be shown to bear upon the act-sit or whose judgments may later define what happened in the situation.

In terms of available research techniques, the investigator

will encounter his greatest difficulty in placing the situation within which the delinquent act occurred in its larger context of neighborhood or community, understood historically. This can be achieved only as the sociogenic case history method and the method of situational analysis are both effectively combined with the method of area analysis described in Chapter 3.

Part of the difficulty may be resolved by operationally defining the variables, especially those that are extrapersonal, to be used in describing the situation. Unfortunately, specifications of situational variables are rarely found in the sociological literature; usually they are only alluded to as a source of further variation. Muzafer and Carolyn Sherif do, however, offer the following list of variables, which is most helpful in the analysis of situational fields and in placing such fields within a larger context:

1. Factors related to individuals involved
2. Factors related to the problem, task, or activity
3. Factors related to the site and facilities
4. Relationships among the preceding three sets of factors

Factors relating to individuals certainly include their age, sex, abilities and skills, their backgrounds, their motives in participating in the situation. They also must include the number of individuals, the homogeneity or heterogeneity of their personal characteristics and backgrounds, the extent and nature of their previous interactions, the existence or lack of established relationships among them, and their attitudes toward the task.

Similarly, the problem or task can be specified in terms of the number of possible alternatives in performance, that is, its degree of structure, and other formal characteristics. But it is equally important to know whether it is new or habitual, easy or difficult for the individuals, how many individuals are necessary for solution, the division of functions required, the relative dependence or interdependence of these functions, and so on.

Similarly, factors related to the site and facilities, such as available space, tools, and the presence or absence or non-participating individuals, do not function independently of the task or of individual factors.[17]

The concept of role may also be most useful in linking the more immediate act-sit to its larger setting. Thus role analysis may be used to clarify the three levels of expectations, giving meaning to the delinquent action situation under examination. The first level involves the broader age-sex role expectations, emanating from the level of the dominant cultural system, that impinge upon the delinquent. The second is the narrower network of subcultural expectations as defined by the lower-class and minority-group identifications of the delinquent. The third level involves the means-ends-conditions-norms relationships[18] as patterned according to the roles of the delinquent actors in their immediate relationships to one another—that is, as members of a common reference group with norms derived from the level of peer group subcultural expectations, as described earlier. The reference-membership group expectations at the peer group level are clearly what the Sherifs mean when they identify the importance of determining the "existence or lack of established relationships" among the actors involved in the act-sit. These reference group expectations define the ends and predispose the delinquent to certain means conditioned by the particular site and facilities. Equally important as conditions operating in the act-sit are the dominant cultural and lower-class and minority-group expectations deemed appropriate for the delinquent. Thus legal norms and subcultural expectations clearly enter the situation as "conditions," but the strength of these expectations will vary in the extent to which they predispose the delinquent to alternative means-ends in the act-sit.

The description of the dominant cultural expectations applied to the delinquent is only one of the conditions necessary for an understanding of on-going, interactive forms of delinquent behavior in any given act-sit. The crucial fact to be determined is the extent to which the delinquent and others involved in the act-sit perceive themselves as participants in or evaluate themselves against dominant cultural expectations *or* are identified more strongly with variant orientations originating at the lower-class and minority-group level, the peer group level, or both. The task then is to determine the relative strength of the delinquent's identifications on all three levels of social expectations.

In obtaining data for situational analysis from existing agency social histories and other records, it must be noted that this information has been gathered almost invariably for purposes related to orientations at the dominant cultural level. The assumptions underlying the development of this level of analysis must clearly guide the interpretation of data provided by official records. A recent methodological work points out that, in attempting any kind of analysis with other people's data, the investigator needs to know not only "what the original collector of available data set out to gather" and the "adequacy of his methods" but he must also be aware of the collector's "definitions of categories." [19] It seems evident that value orientations and other cultural definitions are one set of influences framing official definitions.

The delinquent act represents an infringement of legal norms as defined by dominant cultural expectations, but this fact does not necessarily help to explain the act. It simply defines the act in accordance with the dominant perspective. Situational analysis allows for the possibility of placing the act within the "conduct norms" [20] shared by the residents of a local neighborhood or by members of other indigenous social groups. Situational analysis further allows the observer to see that, even though neighborhood or reference group norms may be shared and accepted within the local milieu, they may be in conflict with the dominant expectations of the larger culture. In fact, the method sensitizes the observer to differences existing between adolescent peer group norms and adult neighborhood norms.

One of the prime methodological difficulties in interpreting delinquent behavioral patterns in their act-sit contexts in terms of prevailing conduct norms stems from the lack of available data in agency records about norms at the lower-class and minority-group subcultural and peer group levels of situational analysis. Since these norms may be at variance with those at the dominant cultural level, the situational analysis method cannot rely exclusively on the customary sources of data derived from the records of middle-class-oriented schools, courts, psychiatric clinics, and related agencies. The method provides for collecting original data on the other two levels of expectation and interpreting this material according to the orientations of the subcultures involved.

An outstanding example of the use of the participant observation technique to obtain such data on adult neighborhood norms and in a local adolescent street corner group is provided in William Whyte's classic study, *Street Corner Society*.[21] Whyte focused on the day-to-day routine activities of young men in a street corner situation in a slum area. By living in the neighborhood he was able to observe, describe, and analyze the groups as they evolved and changed through time. At the outset, Whyte's attention was directed to the amount and duration of contacts between individuals. The underlying assumption with which he began was that the objective description of interaction would provide necessary data on the primary bonds between people and their attitudes toward one another.

Whyte also describes his difficulty in establishing sufficient rapport in the community so that he could gain access to the places where interaction occurred. A settlement house worker suggested a confidant who might provide the necessary relationship with the local community. Whyte describes the role of such an informant, typical of those frequently used by anthropologists in field studies of other cultures:

. . . the head of the girls work program in the Norton Street House understood what I needed. She began to describe Doc to me. He was, she said, a very intelligent and talented person who had at one time been fairly active in the house but had dropped out, so that he hardly came in anymore. Perhaps he could understand what I wanted and he must have the contacts that I needed.[22]

Whyte, through his "informant," was able to find an acceptable place to live in the community, provide a plausible explanation for his presence there, and acquaint himself with the local norms. Thus he was able to fit into the community with the least possible disturbance of its existing patterns.

This method of participant observation is used: (1) in situations when more direct data collection methods would disrupt the process of social interaction; (2) when the persons involved would not be reliable as direct sources of data due to inability or to unwillingness to communicate the necessary information; and (3) for the additional purpose of being able to get more of *the total situation,* rather than isolated, discrete aspects of behavior.

While the problems of the observer role, either participant or nonparticipant, using structured or unstructured categories, are difficult from the standpoint of obtaining valid and reliable information, they are not insurmountable. The method is the best developed to date for obtaining *direct evidence* of the effects of adult and adolescent subcultural expectations on delinquent behavior.

A second important contribution to the methodology of situational analysis, as in the sociogenic case history, is found in the use of local informants. Amplification of the point is found among the work of cultural anthropologists, such as Melville Herskovits[23] and Benjamin Paul.[24] Herskovits makes a further important methodological point in cautioning against the use of either observation or informants as the sole data-gathering technique. He recommends the use of both.[25] The method of situational analysis suggests that the use of informants and observation techniques are as important in studying various subcultures in American society as they are in obtaining information about the cultures of primitive or foreign societies. These data should also enable the investigator to describe the immediate setting within which the delinquency act-sit arose. The task, difficult as it may be, is then to relate this setting to the local neighborhood and the neighborhood in turn to the ecological development of the larger community.[26]

All of this can best be accomplished in the individual case through the use of the sociogenic case history method and the method of situational analysis, as both are combined with the method of area analysis. The companion volume to this book,

Case Studies in the Analysis of Delinquent Behavior, presents three case histories of delinquents prepared in this manner.

Situational Methodology in the Analysis of Delinquency Cases

Case materials about delinquents will be presented in this section to illustrate situational analysis, particularly insofar as this method bears on explanations of why delinquent behavior occurs.

The case of Pedro F., previously discussed in the Introduction, makes the point of situational analysis nicely. This boy was a lower-class Puerto Rican migrant whose people were farmers of a type known as stubborn *jibaros*. Following Queener's principles as previously discussed, these status characteristics alone should have alerted authorities not to apply middle-class standards in their attempts to understand and relate to this adolescent. Thus, from the standpoint of situational analysis, the first significant step is placing the delinquent in the context of his ethnic origins and specifying his particular socioeconomic status *within* his ethnic subculture.

The following verbatim statements from the available official records about Pedro illustrate attempts by agency personnel to explain this boy and his delinquency from the perspective of dominant society—that is, from the dominant cultural level.

(*Probation Officer's report*)

He is seen as an extremely hostile and aggressive boy who has no controls or proper judgment. The gun [involved in one of his offenses] we feel can be psychologically reconciled as a similarization [sic] of a defected super ego. Apparently the boy still continues to suffer from rearable [sic] conflicts which have never been resolved.

(*Psychiatrist's report*)

The projective data suggest that he is unable to respond spontaneously in an emotional situation. He tries to control by regressive techniques. He has an inadequate self-concept and acts out his difficulties with authority figures. His feelings of inadequacy produce hostile impulses, insecurity, and disorganizing destructive behavior.

(Social Caseworker's report)

His delinquency is understandable in terms of his coming from a deprived background, having a poor self-image, lacking in self-confidence, being frightened, and immature in object relationships . . . immaturity in object relationships means the boy does not know how or understand how to give and communicate with others. He cannot relate deeply on an emotional level in such a manner as to have the relationship satisfying to himself and others.

Such interpretations are highly individualized. Little consideration is given to any interpretations which employ analyses other than a strictly psychological one of a type commonly used by correctional agencies. Their psychological explanation contrasts markedly with data obtained first through participant observation and separate interviews with Pedro and then with his friends in their own neighborhood which bring into play utilitarian interpretations at the adolescent peer group subcultural level:

INTERVIEWER: José [one of Pedro's older friends], do you have any idea why he [Pedro] would have been carrying a gun?

JOSÉ: I don't know, Pedro always say, "what if guys come after us and we ain't got nothing to protect us?"

INTERVIEWER: Pedro said he was in East Harlem once and some Italian fellows pulled a gun on him and told him to get out of the area. Were you with him that time?

JOSÉ: No, I was never with him when that happen.

EDDIE [another friend]: I can understand that. Maybe it did happen. It has happened to me. I wasn't the one with Pedro. But, if it did happen, I can see why he might want to carry a gun.

INTERVIEWER [to Pedro himself]: Could you tell me why you had the gun?

PEDRO: For protection, like the others. If they have blades and guns and if you don't have 'em you're down. If you have 'em, you don't have to be afraid of nobody.

It is apparent from this illustration of situational analysis that the meaning of possession of a gun varies considerably with the level from which the act is interpreted. To the actor (Pedro) the gun had a utilitarian value as a weapon in a hostile environment. This was verified by the actor's adolescent peers. Pedro had a history of street fighting and of having been violently attacked. He had also seen his mother and his friends attacked. But these variables find no place in the official versions of this boy and his gun. Officially, Pedro's possession of a gun was symptomatic of his personality defect.

A further example from the case of Pedro F. may serve to clarify the utility of situational analysis in the study of delinquent behavior. The question here concerns the meaning of an encounter between Pedro and a woman teacher in the public school he attended. In describing the encounter, a description of some of the essentials of the action situation and the school setting in which it occurred is also provided.

PEER GROUP SUBCULTURAL LEVEL

(Research interview with Pedro himself)

INTERVIEWER: Art, José and Ana [friends of Pedro] mentioned something else. I wonder if you could tell me something about it. They mentioned some fight with a teacher. Do you remember that?

PEDRO: Was when he grab me and twist my arm and I swung at him. Then he take me to the office of the principal and they say I am on probation and hitting a teacher is bad especially for a boy on probation. But I tell him I don't care and I'm gonna get him anyway.

INTERVIEWER: You are talking about a man teacher. Was there a woman teacher involved also?

PEDRO: Yeah, she is the one that starts everything. I was talking across the room to my friend's sister, and the teacher yells at her and tells her to stop, and she tells the teacher, "so why don't you tell him to stop and not me?" And the teacher she starts yelling at me and saying things I didn't like, and I got mad. And I stood up and went toward her and this other teacher he come in, . . . and he grab me and twist my right arm. I swung at him. And I tell him I ain't doing nothing and he have no right to twist my arm that way.

INTERVIEWER: What had the woman teacher said that made you mad?

PEDRO: She say bad things about my mother and I don't let anybody say bad things about my mother and I went after her and that's when the other teacher come and grab me.

(Research group interview with Pedro's wife and friends)

INTERVIEWER: Eddie, before you go, could I ask you if you know how Pedro got into trouble?

EDDIE: The first time it was with a teacher. He had trouble with a teacher.

ANA [Pedro's wife]: He shook her, you know. Like this [gesturing]!

INTERVIEWER: You mean he actually roughed her up?

ANA: Not so much. Nothing bad. You know. He took her by the shoulders and shook her.

INTERVIEWER: Ana, do you know what happened? Why he did it? Were you there?

ANA: No, but my girlfriend was there. She and Pedro was talking. They was just talking, and the teacher, she start saying things to Pedro, like his mother ain't got no manners and ain't a good woman and things. And he just get mad, that's all.

INTERVIEWER: Do you know the teacher, Ana?

ANA: Yeah, but she ain't there no more. She was a new teacher. The kids didn't like her.

JOSÉ: You know, some of the teachers, they don't like Puerto Ricans or colored and things like that, and they say things or show you they don't like you. She was a teacher like that.

DOMINANT CULTURAL LEVEL

(Probation Officer's report)

On 1/16/6— the boy was again in Court for allegedly striking a teacher and using vile and indecent language at her, calling her very profane names.

(*Institutional case record*)

On 1/16/6—the youngster threatened to strike a woman teacher with his clenched fist. He also used vile and indecent language.

(*Institutional case record*)

Pedro appeared in Intake with Ptl. Frank _____ of the Youth Squad and complainant teacher at P. S. _____ who alleged that on 1/16/6— in P. S. _____, Room 307, Pedro approached her as if to strike her with his clenched fists when he was stopped by another teacher. Boy also used vile and obscene language at her.

(*Probation Officer's report*)

Probation Officer discussed the situation with boy in the Intake office. Pedro related that he was having an argument with a girl and admitted the altercation became rather loud. The teacher told him to stop, said something about his mother, and he admitted using profanity. The youngster stated he cannot control his temper sometimes. Probation Officer got the impression he is still reacting impulsively.

Little of the dynamics of the act-sit, or its school setting as reported from the peer group subcultural level, comes through in the official version of the Pedro-teacher incident. No sense of a crisis situation, in which the teacher herself may have played an important precipitating role, is addressed by the dominant cultural level of analysis. This is clearly suggested in the peer group description. Again, at the dominant cultural level, the description of what happened and why is entirely loaded on the boy and, in this instance, his impulsive nature. In a word, what the teacher probably did is not mentioned, while Pedro is faulted by the official version which considers his behavior removed from the context within which it occurred.

To correct for this distortion, the description and analysis of a delinquent act should make use of *primary data*. Such data are defined as those which originate from the context in which the act occurred, as reported by persons intimately involved and identified with the delinquent, as well as by the delinquent himself. This information must be obtained directly, without being filtered through secondary sources. In the study of delinquent acts, complainants, police officers, schoolteachers, and similar "outsiders" are almost invariably secondary sources. Caseworkers and psychiatrists, as they typically relate to delinquents in courts and other agencies, are also secondary sources and cannot usually be relied upon to give the primary data necessary for situational analysis. Most of what they present is based on their interpretations of what happened and why it happened; little raw data, as such, are reported.

Several factors prohibit such authorities from serving as reliable sources of primary data. Instead of being intimately involved and identified with the delinquent, they are usually considerably removed from him and his interests. In addition to the barrier of age, there is often considerable social distance present arising from differences in social class and ethnic affiliation and identification.[27] As employees of law enforcement, judicial, correctional, and related "helping" agencies, they are typically trying to apprehend, restrain, correct, or change delinquents. While it is not impossible for workers employed by such agencies to develop empathic relationships with delinquents, such relationships cannot be developed easily or simply presumed. Unfortunately, the goals and functions of law enforcement, corrections, and related agencies frequently appear to impede successful empathy between delinquents and workers employed by such agencies. Finally, the official language used to describe incidents in which delinquents are involved and the conceptual frame of reference ordinarily used to describe delinquents themselves and why they did what they are supposed to have done are products of dominant interests and bound by dominant cultural norms, values, and perceptions. These descriptions and explanations superimpose, as it were, special meaning on the events and individuals under scrutiny. As discussed in the Introduction, the total picture about delinquents and their behavior that emerges from these sources is almost entirely negative. In considering delinquents and their behavior outside of their social-cultural contexts, the picture obtained usually stands in sharp contrast to the descriptions and explanations provided by the delinquents themselves and by those closely identified with them.

To succeed in obtaining primary data for situational analysis, the investigator, through field observation and interview, must not only use appropriate sources and cross-check them one with another, but he must also try to identify with the delinquent himself in order to determine as accurately as possible the meaning which the delinquent act had for the youth. Such identification requires the ability to suspend judgment and to put oneself in the place of the delinquent, to literally take his role, in order to see, through the delinquent's eyes, the act-sit in which the delinquency occurred. As Cottrell puts it: "Perhaps the most important methodological implication (of situational analysis) is the one calling for skills by which an investigator can assimilate himself to the acting perspective of his subject, individual or group." [28]

The validity and usefulness of primary data for situational analysis obtained from the delinquent himself, or from those closely associated and identified with him, are likely to be sharply challenged by many of those acting for or functioning out of the dominant cultural level. The arguments used in such challenges usually range from one extreme, which states that the delinquent and those close to him are simply lying, to the other, which maintains that the delinquent's behavior can be understood only in terms of his psychopathology. This controversy is highlighted by the sharp juxtaposition of different levels of interpretation revealed by the method of situational analysis. The issue, unfortunately, cannot be resolved simply and with certainty either on the level of common sense or on that of scientific proof. Acceptance of one interpretation of human behavior rather than another is a complicated human process which depends ultimately upon the cultural tradition to which the practitioner or the scientist belongs. Most agency personnel involved with the delinquency problem have grown up in an occupational or academic and professional culture in which the dominant cultural interpretations mentioned above were taken for granted, and this cultural level has been reinforced by a wide range of interests which have now become associated for them with the "established" interpretations. Official delinquency generally involves socially disadvantaged adolescents whose behavior is often viewed as a serious threat to dominant values and interests. On the professional level, the proposal of a radical new method represents a threat both to professionals and to many in the larger community who may perceive their interests as depending on the continuation of the established interpretations. As a result, competing theories prevail or decline not only on the basis of scientific evidence or proven validity, but also on the basis of cultural and political acceptability. It is not surprising, therefore, that the validity of the method of situational analysis is not apt to be easily accepted by established groups and their representatives. This is not an indication of its defectiveness as a method; it is an example of understandable cultural or political resistance.

Some of the program implications arising out of this resistance, as well as other practical implications of the total assessment methodology presented in this book, will be discussed in Chapter 5. Here it is sufficient to note that the development of new, bipartisan, structural strategies may be needed before situational analysis techniques can be introduced into judicial, correctional, and related processes. These strategies may become essential if established agencies prove incapable of developing empathic relationships with delinquents and unable to incorporate the techniques of situational analysis into existing programs.

Perhaps the significance of the situational analysis method in the study of delinquency can be more easily grasped by a case summary which, unlike that of Pedro F., is not concerned directly with either the issue of dominant-minority-group conflicts or the question of the legitimacy of cultural differences. The case of Bill C. involves an Irish-American youth who apparently was from a middle-class family when he came into conflict with the law. Over a period of six months this adolescent appeared in Family Court on several occasions after he had been apprehended for: (1) seriously stabbing another youth; (2) carrying a loaded zip gun; and (3) riding in a stolen automobile. Only after this third incident did the court decide that he should be committed to a training school with the psychiatric diagnosis of "adjustment reaction of adolescence, with indication of underlying pathology." Prior to this, as is documented by the full-length sociogenic case study of this youth, the court reacted to the stabbing as "an accident." Three months later, when Bill was apprehended intoxicated and carrying a loaded zip gun in the subway, he was sent for psychiatric study. The court's reaction may have been influenced by the fact that, in the course of being apprehended, Bill's zip gun had somehow gone off, discharging its shotgun charge harmlessly. It was after this episode that the psychiatric study was ordered. Subsequent to this, while on parole awaiting disposition after the subway incident, Bill was found riding in a stolen automobile, placed in detention, and later committed to a training school.

During the entire period of more than three years in which Bill was in contact with the court and the training school, authorities considered him to be a youth from a middle-class home and neighborhood. His physical "good looks," verbal and agreeable manner, high intelligence, intact home, and reasonably good educational adjustment lent credibility to this conclusion. Bill's correctional dossier is replete with data and inferences gathered at the level of the dominant culture in support of this view. Almost without exception all authorities saw this boy as middle class.

At the training school some concern was evidenced over his poor academic performance, which did not measure up to the standards necessary for college entrance. Even greater concern resulted when, while on weekend leave home shortly after his sixteenth birthday, Bill was again found with a stolen automobile. Essentially, however, he was still defined as a middle-class youth with a great deal of "potential," in sharp contrast to the usual lower-class and minority-group adolescents from New York City resident at the training school. The descriptions of Bill provided by his parents, who themselves were quite middle class, were entirely consistent with this official view. To both authorities and his parents Bill's delinquency made little sense, except possibly as evidence of his psychopathology. This conclusion was slightly modified as Bill began to adjust to his lengthy stay in the training school. The caseworker there began to see Bill's father as not quite capable of carrying out what was perceived to be his proper father role as a "strong male figure." At this point, Bill's failing began to be defined more and more as a "character weakness" requiring firm masculine guidance from male figures relating to the boy at the school who could provide the necessary "structure" in his life which presumedly his "weak" father had never been able to provide. The father himself, of course, was never consulted about this later interpretation.

Almost nowhere in the long official case history on this youth are there any data gathered from the peer group subcultural level. Hardly any data in the official record relate Bill's delinquent episodes to the social-cultural contexts in which they occurred. Only when the research staff subsequently reviewed Bill's case was it possible to see more clearly the reference group influences actually present, the specific settings and general neighborhood within which the boy's delinquent acts had unfolded, and the meaning these acts had for the boy in providing status satisfactions for his pressing personal needs.

Data from the peer group subcultural level revealed that Bill was only in some ways a middle-class youth. In a very real sense, he was still a working-class youth, whose family had only recently moved from a low-income housing project to a new high-rise apartment in a nearby middle-class neighborhood.[29] Bill kept returning to his old neighborhood in his free time because, for him, that was still where the "action" was. It was there that he enjoyed considerable freedom from his family's supervision, the pleasure of his old friends, and the fun of drinking, and otherwise "living it up." And it was there, in his old neighborhood, that the stabbing incident occurred, in the course of a rather ordinary street fight between rival adolescent factions on St. Patrick's Day night. It was there, too, that Bill began to make and sell zip guns to other adolescents. And it was there, finally, that he began to develop a reputation which he enjoyed as a "wild one" who was not to be crossed and who should be looked up to by other adolescents. Automobile "joy-riding" was a common practice in this neighborhood, as were drinking and general hell-raising. None of these facts was evident, however, until after the primary data required by situational analysis at the peer group level were developed. Only then could it be seen that Bill's deep desires for personal recognition were being met by his performance of the delinquent roles made available to him in his old neighborhood.

Conclusion

The theoretical orientation which the new assessment methodology presented in this book is designed to apply insists that the essential task in the study of delinquency causation is to explain delinquent *acts* in terms of the *motivational-situational-cultural complexes* within which they occur. The *sociogenic case history* method, which constitutes the first essential of this methodology, was described in Chapter 1. The present chapter described the method of *situational analysis,* which is the second component of the new methodology. The final component, the method of *area analysis,* will be presented in the next chapter.

The thrust of situational analysis is to relate specific acts of delinquency to the concrete on-going situations in which they occur. In carrying out this function, it becomes apparent that situational analysis tends to produce data about and interpretations of delinquency which often run counter to official descriptions and interpretations of such behavior. Some of the complications this contradiction raises for carrying out the new methodology will be considered in concluding sections of this book. At this point, it is perhaps sufficient to state that investigators should not disdain to ask direct questions of delinquents and those who know them well about why they committed their delinquent acts. By such judicious questions the investigator can strive to bring some measure of balance into a field where, at present, so many trained professionals tend to assume that the motivation in delinquency is essentially unhealthy and a product of some form of psychopathology.[30] The careful investigator can in this way develop explanations of delinquency which increasingly relate and merge the total set of forces involved in such behavior.

References

1. Howard S. Becker, *Outsiders: Studies in the Sociology of Deviance.* New York: Free Press, 1963.

2. Kurt Lewin, *Dynamic Theory of Personality.* New York: McGraw-Hill, 1935, p. 41.

3. David Krech and Richard S. Crutchfield, *Theory and Problems of Social Psychology.* New York: McGraw-Hill, 1948, Chap. 1.

4. Theodore M. Newcomb, Ralph H. Turner, Philip E. Converse, *Social Psychology.* New York: Holt, Rinehart and Winston, 1965, pp. 1–10.

5. Leon Festinger, "A Theory of Social Comparison Processes," in Alexander P. Hare, Edgar F. Borgotta, and Robert F. Bales, *Small Groups.* New York: Knopf, 1965, pp. 163–182.

6. Richard R. Sears, "Social Behavior and Personality Development," in Talcott Parsons and Edward A. Shils, *Toward a General Theory of Action.* Cambridge, Mass.: Harvard University Press, 1951, pp. 465–478.

7. Harry Stack Sullivan, "Socio-Psychiatric Research: Its Implications for the Schizophrenia Problem and for Mental Hygiene," *American Journal of Psychiatry* 10:977–991 (May 1931); Harry Stack Sullivan, *Conceptions of Modern Psychiatry.* Washington, D.C.: William A. White Foundation, 1947.

8. W. I. Thomas and Florian Znaniecki, *The Polish Peasant in Europe and America,* 2 vols. New York: Dover Publications, 1958. This work was originally published in 1918.

9. Talcott Parsons, *The Social System.* New York: Free Press, 1951.

10. Leonard S. Cottrell, Jr., "Analysis of Situational Fields in Social Psychology," *American Sociological Review* 7:370–382 (June 1942).

11. Theodore R. Sarbin, "Role Theory," in Gardner Lindzey, ed., *Handbook of Social Psychology*. Cambridge, Mass.: Addison-Wesley Publishing, 1954, I, 251–253.

12. Becker, *op. cit.,* Chaps. 8 and 9.

13. The concept "reference-membership groups" is utilized to denote groups whose norms are used as anchoring points in structuring the perceptual field, rather than the notion of comparison groups or groups to which the actor aspires. See Muzafer Sherif, "The Concept of Reference Groups in Human Relations," in Muzafer Sherif and Milbourne O. Wilson, *Group Relations at the Crossroads*. New York: Harper & Row, 1953.

14. Newcomb, Turner, and Converse, *op. cit.,* p. 68.

15. For a discussion of the need for this type of approach in the study of mental illness, see John A. Clausen and Melvin L. Kohn, "The Analysis of Ecological and Statistical Distribution of Personality Variables," *American Journal of Sociology* 60:140–151 (September 1954).

16. Llewellyn Queener, *Introduction to Social Psychology*. New York: Sloane Associates, 1951, p. 6.

17. Muzafer Sherif and Carolyn W. Sherif, "Varieties of Social Stimulus Situations," in S. B. Sells, ed., *Stimulus Determinants of Behavior*. New York: Ronald Press, pp. 82–83.

18. For a brief discussion of these relationships, see John M. Martin and Joseph P. Fitzpatrick, *Delinquent Behavior: A Redefinition of the Problem*. New York: Random House, 1965, p. 172.

19. Claire Selltiz, Marie Jahoda, Morton Deutsch, and Stewart W. Cook, *Research Methods in Social Relations*. New York: Holt, Rinehart and Winston, 1964, pp. 4–5.

20. "Conduct norms" are discussed by Thorsten Sellin, "The Conflict of Conduct Norms," in Marvin E. Wolfgang, Leonard Savitz, and Neil Johnson, eds., *The Sociology of Crime and Delinquency*. New York: Wiley, 1962, pp. 226–229.

21. William F. Whyte, *Street Corner Society*. Chicago: University of Chicago Press, 1943.

22. *Ibid.*, p. 290.

23. Melville J. Herskovits, *Man and His Works*. New York: Knopf, 1950, pp. 86–87.

24. Benjamin D. Paul, "Interview and Field Techniques," in Alfred L. Kroeber, ed., *Anthropology Today*. Chicago: University of Chicago Press, 1953, p. 447.

25. Herskovits, *op. cit.*, p. 87.

26. Clausen and Kohn, *op. cit.*

27. An earlier discussion of such barriers in casework with delinquents is contained in John M. Martin, "Social-Cultural Differences: Barriers in Casework with Delinquents," *Social Work* 3:22–25 (July 1957).

28. Cottrell, *op. cit.*, p. 372.

29. For a brief discussion of this type of upward mobility as a more general explanation of delinquency among some parts of the middle class today, see Martin and Fitzpatrick, *op. cit.*, pp. 60–61.

30. For a further discussion of this point, see Gordon W. Allport, *Personality and Social Encounter*. Boston: Beacon Press, 1964, Chap. 6.

Chapter 3

THE METHOD OF
AREA ANALYSIS

The Theory and Method of
Area Analysis

Delinquent behavior is best analyzed in the context of
the total social and cultural conditions within which
it occurs as both are situated in time and geographic
space. This principle is a keystone in the demographic
and ecological study of crime, delinquency, and related social problems in urban areas.[1] Closely related
principles which also contribute to a social understanding of deviance are as follows: persistent deviance flourishes best with group support; and deviance
typically has a history in particular locales.[2]

   The relationship of the local community to the
behavior of its residents involves much more than the
delinquency and social control of local youth groups.
Quite clearly, it also appears to involve a variety of
other aspects of neighborhood life, including the role
of local primary groups in the attainment of individual and social goals, and the influences of different
types of neighborhoods on the educational aspirations
of young people. Thus there appears to be a close
relationship between different local environments and
what occurs within them. Based on this principle,

which has a long history in the social science literature, it has been convincingly argued by a few social workers that neighborhood assessment in its own right, as distinct from the psychosocial study of individuals, is essential as a guide to successful social intervention with respect to delinquency and other social problems.[3]

Much more than population statistics and social geography are involved in the successful assessment of urban, high-delinquency areas. In their review of the extensive work done on the "operating milieu" in which delinquency is concentrated, John Martin and Joseph Fitzpatrick state:

> Although some have cited the links of physical blight, geographic isolation, and urban growth to delinquency, the central emphasis in most [operating milieu] theories is on the social and cultural qualities of delinquency-prone neighborhoods and areas, and on the residents' various life situations, problems, and needs which breed such conditions.[4]

The goal of the structural approach presented in this book is to combine demographic and ecological information about delinquency areas with information about delinquents, their behavior patterns, and the social and cultural characteristics of their life situations, in order to understand more completely the delinquency endemic in such areas. The method of area analysis, the subject of this chapter, provides the relevant demographic and ecological information, as well as the specific facts about local conditions, needed to understand a high-delinquency neighborhood. Area analysis also identifies and describes areas of high-delinquency concentration within the context of changing urban communities. The methods of the sociogenic case history and of situational analysis, as described in earlier chapters, provide the particulars about delinquent individuals living in such areas and about their life situations, problems, and needs. These two methods also provide much detailed information about the social and cultural conditions characteristic of such areas as these are experienced and reacted to by residents, particularly by adolescents who have come to official attention because of deviant behavior.

Because the assessment of high-delinquency areas being described places such areas in the historical context of changing urban communities, the methodology also helps to relate the conditions of life in such areas to the broader processes of social change characteristic of the wider community. Martin and Fitzpatrick warn that developing insight into just such relationships is vital if a local, high-delinquency area is to be properly understood. They hold that the study of conditions, social or otherwise, found within the confines of local neighborhoods is insufficient, stating:

> One must also ask: What conditions extending far beyond the confines of any one local area account for the existence of that area? In the concrete: Why does Chicago's Black Belt exist? Why does New York City have its Spanish Harlem or its Little Italy on the Lower East Side? Why does any community have its slums? [5]

The method of area analysis also seeks to provide partial answers to questions of this order.

The method begins with the well-established principle that official rates of crime and delinquency vary widely by country and region, according to urban-rural differences, and according to neighborhood differences within particular cities.[6] No presumption is made that these statistics drawn from the records of law enforcement and other social control agencies reflect the *real* ecological patterning of illegal behavior in the communities studied. Instead, it is assumed that the statistics reflect only those acts of crime and delinquency which have come to official attention and which have been recorded in such a manner that they can be counted. When the statistics are based on the number of individual residents in an area who have been arrested because of law violation, it is also assumed that the ecological patterning of such cases is a highly accurate reflection of the distribution of agency caseloads in terms of time and geographic space. However, unless such offender statistics are computed according to a *rate* per specified number of residents based on a recent census for the appropriate age group, no inferences can be drawn regarding the proportion of offenders to nonoffenders living in an area.

Within the strictures imposed by these assumptions, it remains nonetheless true that some locales have very little *official* crime and delinquency of any kind and very few residents who are *officially* known to enforcement agencies. On the other hand, some areas have high rates all along the line. As Martin and Fitzpatrick interpret these differences:

> The only reasonable explanation for these significant differences, apart from the issues of definition and the relative inability of the poor and otherwise disadvantaged to defend themselves against the official agencies of control, is that the forces giving rise to crime and delinquency of different kinds vary significantly according to area and locale and according to differences in the cultural, social, and personality "systems" characteristic of such ecological variations.[7]

Today a variety of different community action programs are aimed at various ghettos, slum sections, or "gray areas" where urban crime and delinquency, as well as many other social problems, are officially known to be concentrated. All such programs recognize, in a very pragmatic way, this geographic "clustering" of urban problems. The proposed method of area analysis does not compute offender rates for the areas studied. Instead, it describes how the geographic distribution of court-related delinquency cases was determined for the Bronx, one of New York City's five boroughs, during the mid-1960s by simply counting the cases and showing where the delinquents lived. The chapter also describes how the neighborhood site for a community-oriented demonstration program in the delinquency field was selected from among the existing high-delinquency areas identified in the Bronx. Finally, the chapter traces, in both a historical and contemporary sense, population changes in the Bronx, particularly as reflected in the neighborhood selected as the demonstration site.

The various techniques involved in delineating and describing high-delinquency areas make use of established demographic procedures, and no attempt will be made to elaborate upon them here. Even the procedures for "looking over" a neighborhood and discerning its general characteristics, assets, and liabilities and its emerging social issues are now commonly used by community organization workers and others engaged in community action activity. Both approaches to area analysis will be illustrated in the next section.

The use of urban history, as shown later in this chapter, is perhaps not often used in contemporary community studies, but its procedures are fairly easily applied with the help of secondary sources readily available from municipal libraries and historical societies, local universities, community councils, and similar sources. Thus, although the task of studying a large urban area through time may seem at first glance to be formidable, the actual work involves the use of well-established techniques.

Once a local high-delinquency area has been identified and described through the method of area analysis, then it becomes a relatively routine matter to keep the description of that area current by periodically adding new data as it becomes available.

In keeping the description of an area up to date, an annual plot of the geographic distribution of agency cases, originally used to delineate the area, may be used, for example, to adjust periodically the boundaries of the area. Repeated systematically year after year, such plots will continually inform the investigator about the ebb and flow of agency cases across the face of the entire city or county of interest. In this fashion, new high-delinquency areas may be identified and the old ones retained, redefined, or rejected as centers of attention.

The next chapter will combine and interrelate the data about the Bronx demonstration neighborhood obtained by area analysis with that provided by the sociogenic case history method and the method of situational analysis, as both were applied to the study of delinquents and their behavior within the demonstration locale. When the data from all three methods were brought together, they provided an understanding of delinquent behavior in the demonstration neighborhood which could not have been obtained by the use of any one of the methods alone.

Delineating a Neighborhood Site for a Delinquency Community Action Program[8]

The Juvenile Court Community Development Project in New York City[9] was one of the projects which provided data for this book and its companion volume, *Case Studies in the Analysis of Delinquent Behavior*. This project was a two-year demonstration (1966–1968) designed to show the significance of an area-focused, community development strategy for programs in juvenile corrections. The program's aim was to demonstrate how a community-oriented assessment process and program might be formulated for the juvenile court. This meant focusing on a geographic area or neighborhood where delinquents were concentrated, instead of on offenders as isolated individuals drawn indiscriminately from various locales.

Once the decision had been made to launch an area-focused program, the problem of selecting a site and of describing the area in terms relevant to the program became a critical one. The Juvenile Court Community Development Project was centered in the East Tremont section of the Bronx, as shown on Figure 2. The process of selecting and delimiting this area and of deciding that it was, in fact, a recognizable "subcommunity" or "neighborhood" will be described in detail. It was in large part a problem of comparing, combining, and integrating statistical data from numerous and disparate sources in order to locate and describe the areas in the Bronx where juveniles lived who were adjudged to be delinquents or PINS* by the Family Court.

---

* In 1962, the Family Court of New York State underwent marked change. One of the changes was the creation of a new designation, PINS (Person in Need of Supervision), for certain types of youth who were previously handled as delinquents. Paraphrased, the new definitions are as follows: (1) Juvenile delinquent means a person over

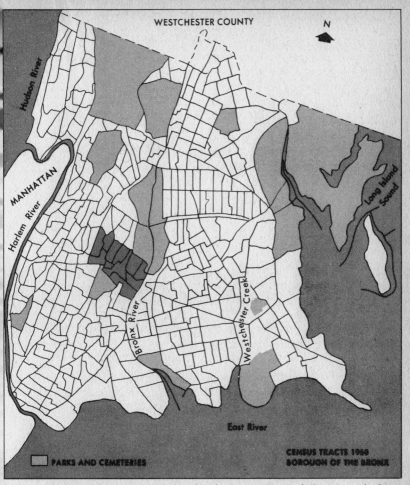

Figure 2. East Tremont Area Within the Bronx, New York City, Juvenile Court Community Development Project, 1966–1968.

seven and less than sixteen years of age who commits any act which, if done by an adult, would constitute a crime; (2) PINS means a male less than sixteen years of age or a female less than eighteen years of age who is an habitual truant or who is incorrigible, ungovernable, or habitually disobedient and beyond the lawful control of parent or other lawful authority.

Location of Juvenile Cases
Referred for Probation Investigation

The geographic distribution of the delinquent population served by the Bronx Office of Probation was determined by plotting on tract maps all adjudicated delinquent and PINS cases referred to that office for social investigation from January 1, 1965 to December 31, 1965. The data for this plot were secured from the record books of the Bronx Branch of the Office of Probation serving the Family Court of New York City, in that borough. To provide some measure of change in these patterns, it was decided that the same plot would also be constructed for all cases investigated from January 1, 1963 to December 31, 1963.* The year 1963 was selected because: (1) it was the first full year of operation following the new Family Court Act of New York State, passed in 1962; and (2) it was close to 1960, the year of the last United States Census which was used in the demographic analysis.

The six areas in which the distribution of 1963 and 1965 cases were highly concentrated are shown in Figure 3.† Each of these six areas was composed of contiguous high-referral census tracts. The six were delineated as possible alternate target areas for the Juvenile Court Project.

The six areas marked off in Figure 3 contain twenty-two

It was decided to include PINS in the enumeration of cases for this project since this label is often applied to boys and girls who have committed delinquent acts and because the specified reasons for its application would usually constitute grounds for a delinquency adjudication in most other jurisdictions.

* Subsequent to choosing the neighborhood site for the Juvenile Court Project in the Fall of 1966, the same plot was made of Office of Probation cases for the year 1966. With but minor variation, the same distribution by area was obtained as in 1965. In 1965 a total of 1,353 cases was involved; in 1966 the number was 1,221.

† It is interesting to note that only half of the tracts contained any cases in either 1963 or 1965. Thus, although the child population of the Bronx is widely scattered over all parts of the borough, Family Court cases referred for probation investigation come from only half of the 374 Bronx census tracts.

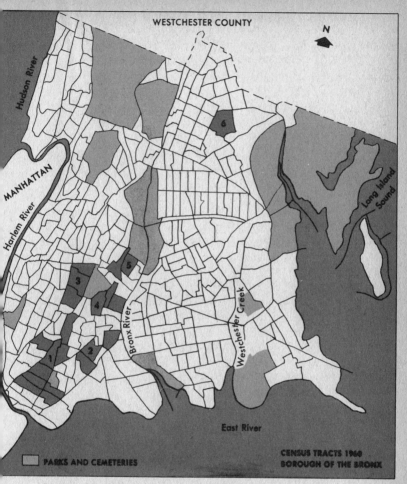

Figure 3. Six Alternate Target Areas, the Bronx, New York City, Juvenile Court Community Development Project, 1966–1968

census tracts representing 5.9 per cent of the total (374) number of tracts in the Bronx. These twenty-two tracts contained a total of 605 cases in 1965, or 44.7 per cent of the total number of delinquent and PINS cases (1,353) referred to the Bronx Branch of the Office of Probation for investigation in 1965. In other words, approximately 6 per cent of the Bronx census tracts, which included approximately 17 per cent* of the target age population, contained approximately 45 per cent of the juveniles referred for investigation to the Office of Probation as delinquents or PINS in 1965. Only one of the six areas experienced less than a 50 per cent increase in cases between 1963 and 1965—Area 6. Area 5 experienced the highest rate of increase—over 200 per cent. This high increase in delinquency suggested that Area 5 was probably experiencing rapid change and that it should be examined more closely as a possible location for the project.

Selected Social and Economic Characteristics of the Bronx and of Six Potential Neighborhoods

As the Bronx census tracts including the largest number of delinquency and PINS cases in 1963 and 1965 were being delineated, the 374 borough tracts were also being analyzed in terms of their social and economic characteristics.

The variables used to characterize the areas were taken from several sources, but the first analysis was based mainly on the census tract reports[10] and some special tabulation of tract data made by the Bureau of Labor Statistics in connection with the President's Committee on Youth Unemployment.[11] The variables were selected on two bases: (1) from empirical evidence, largely the work of Calvin Schmid,[12] that the variables delineated distinct social areas; and (2) from reported empirical studies, which suggested other variables of special relevance to delinquency research.[13]

Two of the best-known typologies devised to provide ana-

---

* This percentage was computed in terms of the total of all Bronx boys, seven through fifteen years of age, and girls, seven through seventeen years of age, who lived in the six high-delinquency areas as reported in the 1960 United States Census. The Family Court Act of 1962 provides New York courts with jurisdiction over delinquents and PINS in these two age groups.

lytic frameworks for studying the social structure of the American city are those constructed by Robert Tryon,[14] and by Eshref Shevky and his collaborators.[15] Both have been used in the analysis of the ecological distribution of crime. Both have also been criticized for lack of a theoretical basis. In exploring the utility of the indices in research on crime, Calvin Schmid and Kiyoshi Tagashira developed a similar set of indices based on the logic of modern statistical techniques.[16] They also found that all their indices, as well as those of Tryon and of Shevky and associates, were highly correlated with a few individual census tract variables. The six variables so described by Schmid and Tagashira were utilized in the present analysis of the Bronx tracts as well as of eight others of special interest to the Juvenile Court Project.

Values for the fourteen variables were computed for each of the tracts in the Bronx with some population in 1960, and these values were converted into quartiles and mapped on tract maps of the Bronx. The clusters of areas which fell into the relevant extreme quartile with respect to any of the variables could be identified, and those with broadly similar social profiles were delimited.*

The six potential target areas and the Bronx as a whole are described in Table 1 for 1960. Of the six potential areas selected on the basis of heavy concentration of delinquency and PINS cases, Area 5 seemed to offer the best potential in terms of a large and increasing number of delinquents. In addition, according to census data for 1960, it was not atypical of the Bronx in terms of the demographic and socioeconomic characteristics of the inhabitants, especially with respect to race and ethnicity. Each of the other areas included proportionately heavier Puerto

---

* Though a more refined analysis might be made using factor analysis to describe more precisely the relationship between delinquency rates and the various social and economic indices, this was not done since the primary interest and need of the project were to compare, in terms of broad social profiles, those areas with high delinquency rates with all others.

Table 1. Selected Social and Economic Characteristics of the Bronx and of Six Alternate Target Areas

Variable	The Bronx	Area 1	Area 2	Area 3	Area 4	Area 5	Area 6
Total Population	1,424,815	82,312	35,014	30,148	31,617	18,795	9,051
Per Cent of Population	100.00	5.78	2.46	2.12	2.22	1.32	0.64
Per Cent Foreign Stock	50.60	30.50	29.30	18.40	31.20	60.50	24.90
Per Cent Negro	11.50	21.70	26.70	30.50	20.30	7.20	42.20
Per Cent Puerto Rican	13.10	34.40	51.40	47.70	41.90	10.10	12.20
Sex Ratio	88.80	89.90	88.00	84.80	89.90	90.50	86.00
Per Cent Males Married Aged 14 and Older	68.20	62.10	64.90	62.10	65.80	67.70	77.10
Per Cent Under Age 16	25.50	29.80	29.30	36.10	29.40	24.30	52.20
Dependency Ratio	503.60	526.90	489.30	654.10	536.30	536.70	1,139.70
Mean Population in Household	3.02	3.24	3.35	3.53	3.30	2.92	4.41

Per Cent Enrolled in School 14–17-Year Group	93.00	83.00	92.00	71.00	87.00	99.00	92.00
Median Grade Completed for Population Aged 25 and Older	9.50	8.60	8.60	7.90	8.40	8.70	10.30
Per Cent Unemployed in Male Civilian Labor Force	4.90	7.20	8.70	8.90	7.40	5.90	6.00
Per Cent Professional and Technical Workers in Male Civilian Labor Force	8.70	3.20	2.60	2.20	3.40	7.10	1.50
Per Cent Moved Between 1955–1960	39.90	37.80	37.30	42.80	39.60	33.60	37.60
Per Cent of Population Moved into SMSA Between 1955–1960	1.87	2.05	2.15	2.33	2.19	1.78	0.78

Rican and Negro populations than the Bronx as a whole. Geo-graphically, in 1960, Area 5 was a kind of "border" or transition area in terms of population composition.

Changes in Population Composition in the Bronx and the Target Area: 1960–1966

The first step in observing the target community in 1966 was a tour of the area by automobile. In this way, the primary and secondary business areas—the centers of larger commercial establishments and the location of smaller neighborhood stores —were identified. Initial observation of the public schools indicated intensive use. Quonset hut facilities suggested overcrowding, and late afternoon dismissals were evidence of double sessions. To the external observer, the housing appeared to be in reasonably good condition. The area is sprinkled by clusters of one- and two-family houses. Puerto Rican and Negro residents were very much in evidence; white residents appeared to be in the older age groups.

Close observation of various blocks in the area and interviews with key personnel from institutions within the area pointed out the nature of this ethnic change. A large part of the East Tremont section had a predominantly middle-class Jewish, Italian, and Irish population until after World War II. Since then, however, it has been in rapid transition, especially during the early 1960s, with Puerto Ricans and increasing numbers of Negroes replacing the older population. One indication of this, for example, is found in the history of the East Tremont YM-YWHA (an affiliate of the Federation of Jewish Philanthropies), which had moved to its present location in the middle of the target area in 1962. By 1966 this organization had decided to give up its location and move elsewhere because of the massive population shift. Four or five synagogues had also closed in recent years.

An attempt was made to determine the extent of the change in the target area by examining school and health statistics and other data collected since 1960 by social agencies, city government, and industry. Because the available statistics did not describe the target area precisely, it was necessary to look at changes in the Bronx as a whole and in whatever smaller sub-areas for which data were available and, from them, to make some inferences as to changes in the target area.

Two sources provided a more recent picture of population change for New York City as a whole and for the boroughs separately. These were the *Population Health Survey* of 1964, conducted by the New York City Department of Health, and the annual estimates of the population of New York City and Westchester County, prepared by Consolidated Edison Company of New York, Inc. The city-wide *Population Health Survey* provided an estimate of the *noninstitutional* population in New York City and the individual boroughs in 1964. The estimate of 7,558,500 from the 1964 survey is about 2 per cent less than the 7,706,300 shown in the 1960 census. According to the survey estimates, Manhattan and the Bronx lost population, Queens and Richmond gained, and Brooklyn remained relatively stable.[17]

The survey results for the Bronx as a whole indicate a drop of 7.4 per cent in the noninstitutional population, resulting from a loss of 18 per cent of the white population other than Puerto Rican, and a gain of 21 per cent and 32 per cent, respectively, in the nonwhite and Puerto Rican populations.

The *Health Survey* findings are not directly comparable with the annual estimates of the population of New York City prepared by Consolidated Edison Company, because the latter focuses on total population changes, compared to the *noninstitutional* population in the *Health Survey*. Con-Edison estimates show a population loss for New York City between 1950 and 1960—particularly of the white component of the population. Between 1960 and 1962, however, according to their estimates, the population remained practically constant, "the composite effect of a continuing but slower decline in Manhattan and Brooklyn, a *slight gain* in the *Bronx* and continuing increase in

Queens and Richmond." [18] By 1963, according to these estimates, the downward population trend had ended and an upward trend, to which all the boroughs contributed, resumed.

"By the end of 1965, continuation of the upward trend established in 1963 had resulted in raising the population of every
borough in the city above the 1960 census figure." [19] The increase appeared to have resulted from a combination of several
short-run factors, such as the World's Fair and a spurt of construction by builders anxious to be covered under the old code,
which was less restrictive than the present one. A slow down-
trend is expected to resume by the end of the decade. For the
Bronx, the estimated gain has been from a total population of
1,425,000 in 1960, to 1,430,000 in 1963 and 1964, to 1,460,-
000 in 1966. The 1966 figure represents a 2.5 per cent increase
over the 1960 census population. The Bronx includes three
"meter districts," or smaller areas for which data are also supplied. Target Area 5 and the surrounding contiguous tracts
which make up most of the East Tremont area are situated in
the northernmost part of District 10 and the southern part of
District 11, both of which show a very low rate of growth compared to District 12, the area east of the Bronx River—0.2 per
cent, 1.0 per cent, and 7.0 per cent respectively. Even with the
overall population growth, the estimated population per occu-
pied dwelling unit was lower in 1966 than in 1960 in all three
Bronx meter districts. This suggests either less crowding of families or the in-migration of single persons and couples with few
children compared to those who left. Nevertheless, an examination of school statistics does not suggest *fewer* children in the
area, but more—a fact which will be discussed shortly. Most
likely there was less crowding because of the restrictions of public housing projects which opened since 1960.

In summary, it appears that the Bronx as a whole experienced either a slight upturn in population trends during the
1960s or at least a diminution in the rate of population decline.
The next section will examine the area in which the project is
situated, as well as the surrounding tracts. The larger area corre-
sponds to what has been historically identified as the East Tre-

mont area of the Bronx; the project was situated in a part of this area.

Target Area 5
and East Tremont

Data on population characteristics for the intercensal period and for areas smaller than the borough are available from only two sources—and from these only indirectly: the Board of Education annual ethnic survey describing the school population, and the Department of Health Annual Vital Statistics report.* Both sources provide information only on ethnic characteristics of the population. Both sources have been used here to get some idea of the extent of population change in the target area.

The school statistics are directly relevant since the clientele in which the Juvenile Court Project was interested were school-age children. The Board of Education estimate of the color and ethnic composition of the school population provides some measure of change in numbers and ethnic composition over time, because most pupils attend schools in the district in which they reside—especially elementary school. Although school district and census tract boundary lines do not generally coincide, an examination of the composition of the school population in schools in and around the target area should also provide an indication of overall population change in the area. Eight such schools were identified and the proportion of pupils listed as "Puerto Rican," "Negro," or "other" was examined each year from 1957 (the first year for which data are available) through 1965. The schools are all situated in that part of the East Tremont section of the Bronx immediately surrounding Area 5.

Between 1957 and 1965 the number of pupils enrolled in all these schools increased—substantially in several cases. The

---

* A long list of persons representing public and private agencies and groups concerned with current population data for New York City was contacted and each indicated that no new data were obtained in the intercensal period except for school and health statistics.

total enrollment figures are shown in Table 2. The increase in enrollment could have resulted from any of several factors: the movement into the area of families with large numbers of children or of families including a larger proportion which sends their children to public rather than parochial schools.

Several of the schools did experience a decline between 1957 and 1962 or 1963, but have increased since then, which suggests that the Con-Edison estimates of the Bronx population, showing a reversal of the downward population trend beginning around 1963, may be a more accurate indicator of what has happened than the Population Health Survey figures for the non-institutional population.

In all the schools in the area, the percentage of pupils who were Negro or Puerto Rican increased, whereas the proportion of "others" declined. With the exception of P.S. 58, which had 51.6 per cent Puerto Rican pupils in 1957, all the schools showed a decline in the "other" population from between two-thirds and four-fifths of the total in 1957 to less than one-fifth in 1965, with the exception of P.S. 57, which still included more than one-fourth "other" in 1965. All this suggests a tendency for younger white families with school-age children to: (1) move out of the area and be replaced by Puerto Rican and Negro families; or (2) not to move into the spaces vacated by older persons dying or moving to smaller quarters.

The school population, which is the age group of primary interest to programs concerned with delinquency, has shifted from a predominance of "other" pupils to a predominance of Puerto Rican and Negro pupils. The increase in numbers in the schools also suggests considerable overcrowding in the public schools.*

---

* The project interviews show that the reverse situation exists in the two local Catholic parochial schools. Enrollment in St. Thomas Aquinas School declined from 886 in 1963 to 684 in 1967. Enrollment in St. Martin of Tours School declined from 1,330 in 1964 to 1,165 in 1966.

Table 2. Total Enrollment in Eight Public Schools of the East Tremont Section of the Bronx, 1957–1965

SCHOOLS	Number of Pupils									Per Cent Change 1957– 1965
	1957	1958	1959	1960	1961	1962	1963	1964	1965	
P.S. 6	962	959	1,001	1,065	1,114	1,148	1,282	1,344	1,604	66.7
P.S. 57	782	810	874	1,005	1,078	1,114	1,168	1,238	1,397	78.6
P.S. 58	545	789	863	921	980	1,002	1,050	1,183	1,080	98.2
P.S. 59	903	908	895	884	923	942	1,112	1,265	1,053	16.6
P.S. 67	1,189	1,124	1,135	1,273	1,423	1,485	1,623	1,864	1,987	67.1
P.S. 92	1,207	1,231	1,257	1,213	1,390	1,498	1,586	1,863	2,021	67.4
J.H. 44	1,060	845	856	838	875	525	1,119	1,120	1,148	12.6
J.H. 118	1,155	1,189	1,102	1,048	970	979	975	1,285	1,300	8.3

Vital Statistics Reports

The Department of Health of the City of New York issues an annual report of vital statistics for New York City as a whole, for the five boroughs, and for health center districts and health areas within each borough. The health areas are the smallest units for which data are available and these usually include several census tracts. All the statistics are reported for the white and nonwhite components of the population. The birth statistics have been further broken down to show the number of births to Puerto Rican mothers. Because the population change in the East Tremont area seems to include a dramatic increase in the size of the Puerto Rican population, this further breakdown was extremely useful in describing the relevant health areas.

The number of births to nonwhite and Puerto Rican mothers was examined and the proportion of the total they represented each year from 1950 to 1964 was computed. The re-

Table 3. Per Cent Nonwhite of Total Live Births in Selected Health Areas of the Bronx, 1950–1964

			Health Areas		
YEAR	17	18	19	20	21.1
1950	1.93	4.67	3.49	3.69	2.95
1951	1.69	5.19	3.54	3.57	3.37
1952	3.32	6.88	5.27	4.58	2.58
1953	4.97	7.60	7.63	4.23	3.54
1954	3.79	10.00	7.90	5.39	3.31
1955	6.43	13.95	9.93	8.06	4.59
1956	10.00	10.81	8.72	10.65	5.82
1957	10.39	17.02	11.70	12.44	3.20
1958	11.89	11.38	12.82	11.72	7.71
1959	14.08	16.42	12.83	12.66	6.54
1960	14.96	13.51	18.21	15.40	11.91
1961	13.39	18.16	21.63	16.34	15.45
1962	21.58	23.54	21.93	18.36	19.37
1963	26.48	30.24	23.82	26.17	22.27
1964	29.65	36.24	28.18	34.14	29.68

sults are shown on Tables 3 and 4. These figures show a continuous increase in the proportion of total births classified as either "Nonwhite" or "to Puerto Rican Mothers," except for Area 18, which shows a continuous increase in the proportion of nonwhite but a decline from a high point of 62 per cent "to Puerto Rican Mothers" in 1960 to 49 per cent in 1964. This may be an area where a Negro population is currently displacing the Puerto Rican population.

Part of this change is probably due simply to a difference in the age structure of the population. That is, the Puerto Rican and Negro population may well be considerably younger than the white non-Puerto Rican population. However, the change in percentages of total births which were nonwhite or to Puerto Rican mothers between 1950 and 1964 is too great to be explained solely by age differences. Again, the data suggest a shift in population composition with respect to ethnicity—from an

Table 4. **Per Cent of Total Live Births to Puerto Rican Mothers in Selected Health Areas of the Bronx, 1950–1964**

| YEAR | Health Areas | | | | |
	17	18	19	20	21.1
1950	1.93	7.16	1.16	2.37	.98
1951	2.91	13.49	2.43	4.08	2.36
1952	4.60	17.66	3.89	6.28	3.55
1953	7.18	28.07	5.96	9.52	4.96
1954	6.50	34.24	8.54	11.26	6.62
1955	10.89	38.75	9.09	10.75	8.52
1956	10.50	48.91	12.08	13.31	14.56
1957	14.35	52.97	10.63	13.38	14.74
1958	14.07	56.43	15.38	17.45	15.75
1959	14.55	59.90	18.11	22.96	18.75
1960	20.90	62.23	19.73	26.60	27.97
1961	25.86	61.92	25.42	35.19	39.13
1962	30.21	61.04	30.39	33.15	42.53
1963	24.78	57.08	35.30	40.48	48.46
1964	30.57	48.76	42.04	39.17	48.59

area of predominantly white, non-Puerto Rican families to an area of predominantly Negro* and Puerto Rican families.

Thus the combination of statistics suggests that the population of Target Area 5, which was selected initially as the project site because it did have a heavy concentration of delinquency and PINS cases and yet was somewhat typical of the Bronx as a whole, had undergone considerable change between 1960 and 1966. The population size appears to have remained relatively stable, but the ethnic composition has shifted to a predominance of Puerto Rican and nonwhite families. On the basis of the total intercensal data available about the Bronx and its subdivisions, the Juvenile Court Project site was tentatively expanded somewhat, as shown in Figure 4, with the two tracts of Target Area 5 remaining the "core tracts" for the project's program.

Subsequently, this thirteen-tract area was confirmed as the site for the project. The borders of the eleven tracts surrounding the two core tracts seemed to be the best definition of the outer boundaries of the project area for two additional reasons:

1. The two tracts comprising Area 5 (363 and 365) were bordered by contiguous tracts in which there was little or no rise in the small number of cases referred to the Bronx Office of Probation between 1963 and 1965.† This indicated a stability in the surrounding tracts, in contrast to the two tracts in Area 5 which had a large increase in the number of cases between 1963 and 1965. It indicated also that this stability of the surrounding tracts could be helpfully related to the community development features of the Juvenile Court Project, which would be centrally focused on the two core high-delinquency tracts.

2. There were a number of natural boundary lines to be

---

* Negroes make up most of the nonwhite total—over 95 per cent for the city as a whole.

† Case data about the surrounding tracts were provided by the procedures described in the previous section, "Location of Juvenile Cases Referred for Probation Investigation."

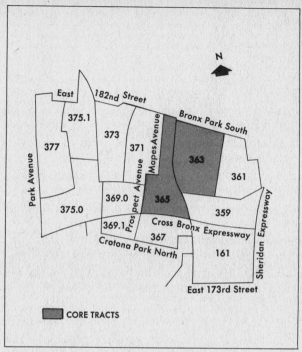

N

CORE TRACTS

Figure 4. Outer Boundaries of the East Tremont Area, Juvenile Court Community Development Project, 1966–1968

considered. On three sides these lines were rather firmly established by Bronx Park South and 182 Street (on the north), by Sheridan Expressway (on the east), and by Cross Bronx Expressway, Crotona Park North, and 173 Street (on the south). Park Avenue was chosen as the western boundary because of the New York Central Railroad tracks which run along it. The ecological enclave between Bronx Park South, Sheridan Expressway, and Crotona Park North has traditionally been called the East Tremont section of the Bronx.

Summary and Conclusions

In summary, the selection of the Juvenile Court Project site was based on the utilization of statistics from the Office of Probation serving the Bronx Family Court, which showed the geographic location and concentration of delinquents and PINS, and on an analysis of census and other data, which provided a description of the social and demographic characteristics of the areas of heavy concentration. Because the entire borough was undergoing rapid change in the years between 1960 and 1966, current data to describe these changes were urgently needed. The changes in size and ethnic composition of the population were documented to some extent by combining available health, school, and public utility data. The analysis was unable to document any change in socioeconomic level, which may also have occurred.

All this suggests ways of utilizing statistics from a number of sources to provide current intercensal descriptions of urban subareas for making intelligent decisions with respect to social action programs. Any kind of community action program and, indeed, many other types of programs, need up-to-date descriptions of their program sites and clientele or target populations. In the intercensal years it is especially difficult to provide accurate current descriptions of small subareas, particularly in rapidly changing urban communities. The present analysis describes one method of making some reasonable estimates of the midcensal social and demographic characteristics of such areas.

Delinquency and Population Changes in the Bronx

Six areas of high-delinquency concentration were found in the Bronx during the mid-1960s. Five were close together, roughly forming a rectangle, in the south-central part of the borough. Area 6, which appeared to be idiosyncratic in ecological terms, lay far to the north and east. This area, a large, low-rent, public housing project, opened in 1953. Area 5, which comprised the two core census tracts of the Juvenile Court Project demonstration site, was on the northern edge of the south-central rectangle.

Three questions may be asked about the ecological distribution of the high-delinquency areas in the Bronx:

—Why do high-delinquency areas in the Bronx form this pattern and not some other?

—How does the emergence of the patterns contribute toward understanding the relationship between Area 5, the core of the demonstration site, and the rest of the Bronx, particularly the remaining high-delinquency areas lying in the south-central rectangle?

—How are future population changes in the Bronx likely to affect the characteristics of the demonstration site?

Answers to these questions should help reveal the forces involved in the sharp increase of delinquency in the Juvenile Court Project demonstration site during the mid-1960s. Such answers may also be helpful indicators of future trends and characteristics in the demonstration area. Moreover, tracing major changes in the Bronx population over the years provides some useful insights into the Bronx of today. These changes are best described in these terms: the south-central Bronx rectangle, 1960–1966; and the total Bronx, 1800–1966.

The South-Central Bronx
Rectangle, 1960—1966

Those familiar with the Bronx know that its population, particularly in the southern part of the borough, is shifting from white to Negro and Puerto Rican. Table 1, in this chapter, suggests that by 1960, among the five areas of high-delinquency concentration in the south-central Bronx, this trend was most advanced in Areas 1–4 which were situated to the south of Area 5. Moreover, as of 1960, in these four areas, and in Area 5 itself, as contrasted with Area 6 off in the northeast quadrant, by far the largest group involved were Puerto Ricans, not Negroes. In fact, as is indicated in the table, although the number of Puerto Rican residents slightly exceeded the number of Negroes in the entire Bronx in 1960, the number of Puerto Ricans greatly exceeded the number of Negroes in the five high-delinquency areas in the south-central rectangle. This was particularly true for Areas 1–4.

Other figures in Table 1 are also instructive. For example, although the 1960 percentage of unemployed males in the Bronx as a whole was close to 5 per cent, the percentage was significantly higher in all five areas in the south-central rectangle. Compared with Area 5, Areas 1–4 to the south had a much higher percentage of unemployed males.

When combined with the information provided in the earlier sections of this chapter about the rapidly changing nature of the population in and around Area 5 between 1960 and 1966, several meaningful conclusions may be drawn about the south-central rectangle: First, the site of the Juvenile Court Project was an interstitial area in rapid transition during the early and mid-1960s. Second, the Puerto Rican and Negro population movements involved in the changes occurring in this area proceeded, and probably still are proceeding, from south to north along a line of advance within the rectangle. This advance has been marked by particular kinds of structural pressures and strains. It is an advance of a new, racially and culturally different population into an already established and densely populated area. It is an advance into an area where physical deterioration has been taking place for many years. Finally, widespread displacement of people and social institutions exists. The political, economic, educational, and other institutions of the area were organized to serve a different population. They now face the difficult task of readjusting to the newcomers; in turn, the newcomers face the difficulty of making these institutions more responsive to their needs. These features give the area the characteristics of an urban frontier. This is what is meant when the site is defined as an interstitial area. If these observations are correct, the demonstration site may be expected to remain a high-delinquency area for some time to come.

The Total Bronx, 1800–1966

The significance of the population changes between 1960 and 1966 characteristic of the south-central Bronx rectangle, and particularly of the central Bronx demonstration site of the Juvenile Court Project, and the relationship of these to increasing delinquency rates can be understood even better if they are viewed in the perspective of the earlier history and growth of the entire borough. Geographical features, technological developments, and, particularly, the building of transportation lines, have converged periodically in the city's history to bring about the movement and often the confrontation of vast numbers of different people. Whenever this movement and meeting of people created an interstitial area as described above, culture conflict, institutional disruptions, and delinquency began to appear. Such areas are better described as differentially organized rather than disorganized, since they are characterized by their own cultural forms and organizational patterns.[20] The direction of these movements can be traced as the city grew.

New York City began at a geographic meeting point of sea and land transport, at the southern tip of Manhattan (see Figure 5). As commerce developed and technology expanded, the city grew from this point as its center along its major transportation routes.

Early immigrants—composed of culturally diverse groups—took part in this movement. Manhattan's East Side has long been divided geographically into a series of ethnic neighborhoods, and the recurrent change in the various sections at moments of tumultuous expansion is legendary in the city's history.[21] Eventually people from these neighborhoods spilled over into other areas, including the southern tip of the Bronx. From there they continued to move northward, following transportation routes which extended up from Manhattan and into the Bronx.

Figure 5. New York City's Five Boroughs, 1968

Manhattan's population in 1800 (60,515) was concentrated in the southern part of the island. To the north the 1800 population was dispersed among a variety of villages. The southern part of Westchester County, which today is the Bronx, had fewer than 2,000 inhabitants, and these were spread through large farm estates in some eighty villages.

By 1900, the population of the Bronx had grown to a hundred times that of 1800. Manhattan and Brooklyn had similarly expanded. In fact, all three of these boroughs had grown in size by merging and then annexing rural village populations. Queens and Richmond, less accessible to the center, increased more slowly and over a greater period of time.

As indicated in Table 5, Manhattan, in a sense, was "filled up" by 1910, reaching its population peak of 2,331,542 in that year. Since then it has shown a rather slow but steady decline. Indications are that a population peak was reached in 1950 for both Brooklyn (2,738,175) and the Bronx (1,451,277).

It is quite possible that New York City reached a population peak in 1960 and that it will not advance much beyond the 7,781,984 total of that year. While further growth is likely in Queens and Richmond, increases in these boroughs will probably occur at the expense of Brooklyn and Manhattan and possibly of the Bronx as well. Queens already appears to be losing residents to its eastern suburbs—that is, Nassau and Suffolk Counties—at only a slightly lower rate than it is receiving new residents from other boroughs. Richmond has been developing since the 1964 opening of the Verrazano-Narrows Bridge, which linked it to Brooklyn, and also since the construction of expressways leading to New Jersey, but Richmond's expansion, too, has been at the expense of other boroughs—Brooklyn and Manhattan. While the Bronx continues to receive population from Manhattan, it seems to be losing people to Westchester, Rockland, and other northern counties. Population shifts, therefore, may increase population in certain segments of the central city, but the overall city population is unlikely to increase very much.[22]

The earlier growth was substantial and perhaps distressing to the small villages which were overrun. However, the general movement was outward into vacant areas and underpopulated sections yet to be politically, socially, and economically organized. Today, to a very large extent, the population movements in the central city involve a different pattern—the invasion of already organized areas, the displacement of older residents and institutions and other kinds of changes which create slums and related interstitial areas.

This becomes very clear if the history of the Bronx is examined more carefully. The Bronx legally became a borough of New York City in 1895. Until then, it had been part of lower Westchester County, wherein towns as such had existed from

Table 5. Population of New York City by Boroughs, Federal and State Censuses, 1790–1960

YEAR	NEW YORK CITY	MANHATTAN	BRONX	BROOKLYN	QUEENS	RICHMOND
1790	49,401	33,131	1,781	4,495	6,159	3,835
1800	79,216	60,515	1,755	5,740	6,642	4,565
1810	119,734	96,373	2,267	8,303	7,444	5,347
1820	152,056	123,706	2,782	11,187	8,246	6,135
1830	242,278	202,589	3,032	20,535	9,049	7,082
1840	391,114	312,710	5,346	47,613	14,480	10,965
1850	696,115	515,547	8,032	138,882	18,593	15,061
1855	907,775	629,904	17,079	216,355	23,048	21,389
1860	1,174,779	813,669	23,593	279,122	32,903	25,492
1870	1,478,103	942,292	37,393	419,921	45,468	33,029
1880	1,911,698	1,164,673	51,980	599,495	56,559	38,991
1890	2,507,414	1,441,216	88,908	838,547	87,050	51,693
1900	3,437,202	1,850,093	200,507	1,166,582	152,999	67,021
1905	4,013,781	2,112,380	271,630	1,358,686	198,240	72,845
1910	4,766,883	2,331,542*	430,980	1,634,351	284,041	85,969
1915	5,047,221	2,137,747	615,600	1,798,513	396,727	98,634
1920	5,620,048	2,284,103	732,016	2,018,356	469,042	116,531
1925	5,873,356	1,945,029	872,168	2,203,991	713,891	138,277
1930	6,930,446	1,867,312	1,265,258	2,560,401	1,079,129	158,346
1940	7,454,995	1,889,924	1,394,711	2,698,285	1,297,634	174,441
1950	7,891,957*	1,960,101	1,451,277*	2,738,175*	1,550,849	191,555
1960	7,781,984	1,698,281	1,424,815	2,627,319	1,809,578	221,991

* Peak Years

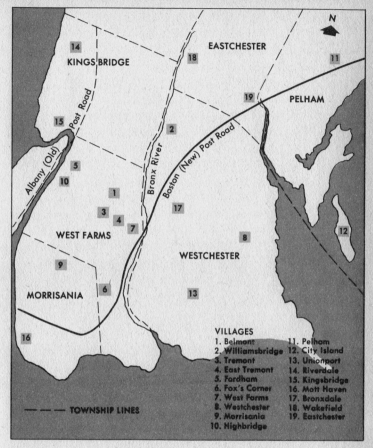

Figure 6. Lower Westchester County (Bronx) Circa 1860, Townships, Major Villages, Major Transportation Routes*

*Locations are approximate, after James Wells, Lewis Hopper, Josiah Briggs, eds., *The Bronx and Its People*, Vol. 1 (New York: Lewis Historical Publishing Co. Inc., 1927), p. 233 ff., and passim.

early colonial times. The Bronx of 1968 was an outgrowth of the seventy-five to eighty villages spread through six townships established in the area more than a hundred years before. Figure 6 shows the locations of some of these villages and describes the approximate boundaries of the six townships. At the time the

Bronx became part of New York City, its population numbered 88,000, as compared to 1,700 persons in 1800, some ninety-five years before.

From earliest times there was some industry in the Bronx: milling snuff at the Lorillard estate; the foundry in Mott Haven; the munitions at Spuyten Duyvil; textile-dyeing and milling at the Lydig; lumber and feed-milling in other villages. These industries, however, were quite sporadic or tied to agriculture. When the Civil War broke out, cotton-milling and textile-dyeing virtually ceased. But already replacing textiles were the goods and services tied in with steel, coal, oil, and electricity. The railroads were built to haul not only the freight of these emerging industries, but also the workers who manned them and whose residences multiplied around them. The Bronx developed after the Civil War largely in response to these industrial changes.

The importance of the transportation lines in this development is clear. Very early in the nineteenth century the New York Central Railroad had linked New York City and Albany with the cities of the Midwest. The Harlem Division of the New York Central, built in 1842, related the early industrial developments in the Bronx to points north and south. During the Civil War this Division grew in importance because it could move men and munitions between Manhattan and parts of what is now the Bronx. By the time of the Civil War, the New Haven Railroad had also been built across the Bronx to link the seacoast cities of New Rochelle, Stamford, Bridgeport, and New Haven with points farther "down East." This rail system was a "tap root" of New York City's external transportation system, joining the city with other urbanizing areas, principally to the north and west, but also to the east. This was the railroad sequence to the Boston Post Road which, for the previous century, had put the East Tremont section of the Bronx on the main route between New York and Boston. Transportation lines made West Farms and East Tremont one of the "meeting places" in the Bronx for the rapidly emerging world outside. It marked it as a place where change would be important and continuous. At the same time, the transportation system was also segmenting and defining areas and land use within the city itself. The western half of Bronx County, lying between the Bronx and Harlem Rivers, is a series of high ridges running north and south. The building of transportation lines and the migration of population related to these lines respected these elementary geographical facts. Both moved south to north along the high ground.

While the railroads brought industry along the Harlem River, they also brought people and industry into the Bronx, pouring thousands into the villages of Morrisania, Tremont, East Tremont, Belmont, and Fordham from 1860 to 1900. When the New York Central opened its second route northward in the late 1860s, its first stops were the villages of Tremont and Fordham. By 1900, these villages had lost their separate identities. At the same time, the Central was also filling up the northern villages of Williamsbridge and Wakefield.

Beginning in 1870, on Manhattan's Lower East Side, and in full operation from lower Manhattan to the upper Bronx by 1900, the Third Avenue elevated railroad had reached into the growing suburbs. By 1886, this "El" was stopping at East Tremont and Morrisania. By 1900, all land in the south-central Bronx, as far north as the former village of Belmont, was developed and heavily populated. Both Morrisania and Tremont were noted, by 1915 to 1925, for their new elevator apartment houses. By 1930, both of these sections were marked by their overcrowding and growing obsolescence.[23]

The "El" transportation system of the city, of which the Third Avenue line was the first major link, continued to expand at an accelerated rate after 1905.[24] Starting that year, the "Els" also went underground.

The tracks of the New York Central, the Third Avenue "El," and the IRT subway all converged northward out of Manhattan toward a central point in the south Bronx of 1905, bringing families for the new fashionable apartment dwellings just north of St. Mary's Park (see Figure 7). The extension of the IRT Pelham Bay line transformed another fashionable village, Pelham Park, into a substantial residential section by 1920. Between 1900 and 1920 the "El" had extended into the northern

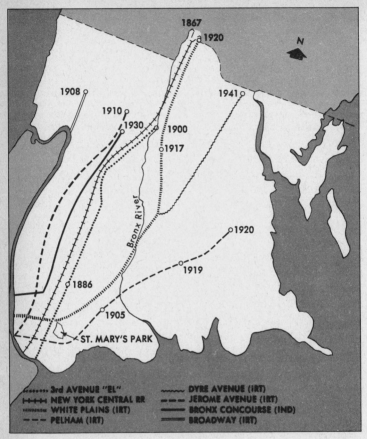

Figure 7. Extensions of Mass Transportation Routes in the Bronx, New York City, by Date of Completion

Bronx, and the IRT subway had opened all the way to the city of Mount Vernon in Westchester County. The Bronx Concourse Independent subway, also extending up into the northern Bronx, was built during the Depression years of the 1930s, in part to relieve unemployment, but also to stimulate population growth and development in the north and west Bronx.

The Broadway IRT subway extended to Kingsbridge by

1908. Ten years later, the Jerome Avenue line running to Wood-lawn was completed, and the Ninth Avenue "El" (since removed) extended across the Harlem River to join it. It served Highbridge, which had already grown from village to urban neighborhood with the building of the Reservoir, the Croton Aqueduct, and the High Bridge Aqueduct during the latter half of the nineteenth century.

The mass transportation system of New York City sorted and distributed the rapidly increasing city population of the period 1880 to 1930. In the Bronx this movement was from south to north, as people moved out of Manhattan, crossed the Harlem River, and followed the expanding mass transit systems up through the center of the Bronx.

By 1930, the Bronx population was well over the one million mark (see Table 5). It reached 1,394,711 in 1940 and peaked at 1,451,277 in 1950. According to the last United States Census, it had declined somewhat to 1,424,815 in 1960.

A special 1966 survey of the Bronx found that its population had increased slightly in that year to about 1,447,000.[25] This gain was somewhat less than, but nonetheless consistent with, the Con-Edison estimates for the borough cited earlier. Thus, in the twenty-six years between 1940 and 1966, the Bronx population has hovered close to 1.4 million.

Until about 1930 or 1940 the great changes in the Bronx population, which had taken place over the previous hundred years, had involved the movement of a steadily expanding population from Manhattan into large sections of open or underpopulated land which was newly built up to receive the newcomers. It was also an essentially all-white population. Even as late as 1940, Negroes numbered only 1.7 per cent of the total Bronx population of 1,394,711, and other races were represented by insignificant numbers. By 1950, however, the number of Negroes in the Bronx had increased to 6.7 per cent, and the Puerto Ricans, the next most significant group, numbered 4.3 per cent. Even more substantial changes had occurred by 1960, when the Puerto Ricans first began to outnumber the Negroes in the Bronx. By that year, Puerto Ricans accounted for 13.1 per cent of the Bronx population, as compared with 11.5 per cent for the Negroes. According to the special survey of the Bronx in 1966, the changes were even more pronounced in that year, with the proportion of Puerto Ricans showing an increase to almost 21 per cent, and that of Negroes to slightly more than 17 per cent. Thus, by 1966, it was estimated that Puerto Ricans and Negroes together constituted about 38 per cent of the total Bronx population.

In sum, for twenty-six years, from 1940 to 1966, the total Bronx population held steady at close to 1.4 million. Most significant, however, is the fact that during the same period the number of Negroes and Puerto Ricans in the Bronx increased from under 2 per cent to about 38 per cent, with the Puerto Ricans outnumbering the Negroes in the borough in recent years.

Summary and Conclusions

The large ethnic changes in the Bronx population, involving the Negro and Puerto Rican newcomers, seem to be following along the same mass transit routes through the middle of the borough from the south to the north as did earlier population movements which have been overflowing from Manhattan during the past century and a half. The major differences, however, are clear. Whereas, during the earlier periods the movement involved whites moving into sparsely populated areas, many of them newly built up, or into sections populated by other whites often of the same ethnic background, the Puerto Rican and Negro migrants to the Bronx in the 1950s and 1960s were moving into already organized, densely populated areas, where real estate was often in incipient decay, and where they were displacing large numbers of well-established whites. Thus these areas began to take on that interstitial character which, at other times and in other places in the city, also involved culture conflict, institutional disruption, differential organization, and delinquency.

This review of population changes in the Bronx, particularly in the south-central rectangle where delinquency was concentrated in the mid-1960s, indicates that recent population changes in the Juvenile Court Project demonstration area reflect the massive shifts in the ethnic composition of the Bronx population. These changes represent a recurrence of the massive shifts of ethnic populations which have periodically occurred elsewhere throughout the city's history. Because of these changes, and the accompanying alterations in the basic fabric of neighborhood life which they bring, the demonstration site may be expected to be a high-delinquency area for some time to come.

Some of the specific consequences of this ecological invasion and succession, which took place in the mid-1960s in the East Tremont site of the Juvenile Court Project, will be considered next. Particular attention will be given to the relationship between the endemic delinquency patterns found in that neighborhood during the mid-1960s and the massive and rapid structural changes in the area resulting from the flood of ethnic change throughout the borough.

References

1. For a summary of various community studies of crime and delinquency in the United States and abroad during the last 150 years, see Terence Morris, *The Criminal Area*. London: Routledge and Kegan Paul, 1958, Chaps. 1–6.

2. David Matza, *Delinquency and Drift*. New York: Wiley, 1964, p. 63.

3. Phillip Fellin and Eugene Litwak, "The Neighborhood in Urban American Society," *Social Work* 13:72–80 (July 1968).

4. John M. Martin and Joseph P. Fitzpatrick, *Delinquent Behavior: A Redefinition of the Problem*. New York: Random House, 1965, p. 74.

5. *Ibid.*, p. 74.

6. Morris, *op. cit.*, Chap. 2.

7. Martin and Fitzpatrick, *op. cit.*, pp. 29–30.

8. Adapted from a paper by Mary G. Powers, entitled, "Utilizing Available Social Statistics to Delineate Program Sites for Community Action Programs," presented at the American Statistical Association Meetings, December 1967.

9. This demonstration project was cosponsored by the Department of Sociology and Anthropology, Fordham University, and the Graduate School of Social Work, New York University. Participating organizations were the Family Court of the State of New York in New York City, and the Office of Probation for the Courts of New York City. The Office of Juvenile Delinquency and Youth Development, United States Department of Health, Education, and Welfare, funded the project. For a more detailed description of this project, see John M. Martin, "The Juvenile Court Community Development Project in New York City," *Criminologica: An Interdisciplinary Journal of Criminology* 5:35–40 (May 1967).

10. *United States Censuses of Population and Housing: 1960 Census Tracts, Final Report, P. H. C. (1)-104, Part 1.* Washington, D.C.: United States Bureau of the Census, 1962.

11. *Income, Education and Unemployment in Neighborhoods: New York City: The Bronx.* Washington, D.C.: United States Department of Labor, Bureau of Labor Statistics, 1963.

12. Calvin Schmid, "Urban Crime Areas: Part I," *American Sociological Review* 25:527–542 (August 1960); Calvin Schmid, "Urban Crime Areas: Part II," *American Sociological Review* 25:655–678 (October 1960).

13. See Kenneth Polk, "Juvenile Delinquency and Social Areas," *Social Problems* 5:214–217 (Winter 1957–1958); Karl Schuessler, "Components of Variation in City Crime Rates," *Social Problems* 9:314–323 (Spring 1962); and Sarah L. Boggs, "Urban Crime Patterns," *American Sociological Review* 30:899–908 (December 1965).

14. Robert C. Tryon, *Identification of Social Areas by Cluster Analysis.* Berkeley, Calif.: University of California Press, 1955.

15. Eshref Shevky and Wendell Bell, *Social Area Analysis.* Stanford, Calif.: Stanford University Press, 1945.

16. Calvin Schmid and Kiyoshi Tagashira, "Ecological and Demo-

graphic Indices: A Methodological Analysis," *Demography* 1:194–211 (1964).

17. "Population Characteristics, 1964" in *Population Health Survey*. New York: New York City Department of Health, April 1966.

18. *Population of New York City and Westchester County*. New York: Consolidated Edison Company of New York, Inc., New York System Engineering Department, September 1966, p. 1.

19. *Ibid.*, p. 1.

20. For a further discussion of this point, see Maurice R. Stein, *The Eclipse of Community*. New York: Harper & Row, 1964, Chap. 5.

21. See Robert Ernst, *Immigrant Life in New York City 1825–1863*. New York: King's Crown Press, 1949. For a later period in the 1890s, see Jacob A. Riis, *How the Other Half Lives*. New York: Scribner, 1902.

22. *Bronx, Manhattan, Brooklyn* [2 vols.], *Queens, Richmond*. New York: The Community Council of Greater New York, Bureau of Community Statistical Services, Research Department, 1965. These six volumes detail each local community in every borough, making largely descriptive use of census population data from 1950, 1955, and 1960.

23. See Gilbert Tauber and Samuel Kaplan, *The New York City Handbook*. Garden City, N.Y.: Doubleday, 1966, pp. 504–522.

24. For a detailed description of the development of New York's electric railroad system, see pamphlet by Herman Rinke, *Fifty Years of Millions!* New York: Electric Railroaders Inc., 1954.

25. *A Profile of the Bronx Economy*. New York: Institute of Urban Studies, Fordham University, July 1967, p. 14.

Chapter 4

DELINQUENCY AS A CONSEQUENCE OF STRUCTURAL CHANGE

Definitions of delinquency and programs to prevent and control such behavior are political affairs; they operate within a system of law, but they are subject to all the forces of power at work in complex social systems. From the social point of view, delinquency involves three elements: (1) endorsement of a value by a politically important group; (2) conflict from within or from outside the group by others who do not subscribe to this value and who, in fact, seem to endanger it by their actions; and (3) a calculated, sometimes compassionately applied, effort by those who uphold the value to coerce those who violate or ignore it.[1] To a major degree, then, what is called delinquency and what is done about it depend upon who holds the power. As defined here, power means the ability of a group to organize, to act decisively, and to get what it wants.

Consider, for example, how different the definition of what constitutes delinquency would be if members of what Gunnar Myrdal has termed the American "underclass" were in control of legislative and law enforcement processes. It is not likely that

members of this interest group would call as much of the behavior of their children delinquency as is presently so called
by officials, nor is it likely that the youngsters would as readily
be shipped off to training schools and reformatories for cor-
rective purposes.

The impotency of this underclass to protect its children
from such treatment is today more apparent than ever. Relationships between the most disadvantaged lower-class members and
the larger society are worsening. Riots and other civil disorders
have marked the ghettos of American cities, which are increasingly becoming concentrations of lower-class Negroes and other
disadvantaged minority-group peoples who are angry and rebel-
lious at being left behind in the long national surge toward affluence *and* influence. The white community has responded with
force and with preparations to act with even greater force to
meet future disorders, but with little else. Basically, nothing has
changed, except that attitudes have hardened on both sides. Such
polarization works a classic conflict of interest into a set of
structural relationships which have always been difficult and
marked by tension and strain.[2]

It is clear that the social definition of crime and delinquency is essentially political. A striking illustration of this, in
another area of American life, can be seen in the authorities' handling of public dissent against national involvement in the Vietnam war. College students have been arrested, military officers
courtmartialed, and older intellectuals convicted because of their
open defiance and resistance to federal policy. Obviously, a dis-
tinctly different social type of "criminal" is involved in this resistance than is ordinarily encountered by the police and in the
courts. A few of these dissenters are nationally prominent men
of substantial reputation. Most are otherwise considered highly
respectable by the community at large. Nevertheless, all have
been labeled "deviant" for acting contrary to the rules laid down
and upheld by those who wield ultimate national power. Moreover, as with the race riots, the new deviancy is itself motivated by ideological interests. Thus, as Irving Horowitz and
Martin Liebowitz have suggested, the new deviancy is not only

collective behavior, it is also highly political, organized, and purposeful behavior. Such behavior is obviously a far cry from conventional deviant acts as theft, assault, and homicide, which are committed by individuals acting alone or in small groups for apolitical reasons.[3]

In writing about the social meaning and relativity of so-called deviance, Howard Becker[4] charges that deviance is "created by society," stating:

> . . . I mean . . . that *social groups create deviance by making the rules whose infraction constitutes deviance,* and by applying those rules to particular people and labeling them as outsiders. From this point of view, deviance is *not* a quality of the act the person commits, but rather a consequence of the application by others of rules and sanctions to an "offender." [5]

Looking at deviance in this light makes it necessary, therefore, for the scientist to specify the group and the standards upon which the judgment of deviance is based. In this context, when the scientist applies the label "deviant" to a social behavior pattern, he merely indicates his recognition of the fact that the item in question is judged to be deviant by some other group. Recognizing the existence of such judgments becomes particularly important when the normative standards against which the behavior is measured are those of the middle class, whose political position in the American social structure is such that it is able to impose sanctions upon those individuals and groups who deviate from its standards. These sanctions, both formal and informal, may profoundly affect the individual's social life and psychological condition. When the behavioral patterns judged deviant by middle-class standards are associated with a particular group in the society, such as lower-class Negroes, Puerto Ricans, or Mexican Americans, the sanctions imposed can significantly alter that group's relationships to conventional institutions.[6]

It should also be noted that delinquency is a specific form of deviance. For delinquency, the definitions used in forming judgments are articulated in the statutes of the state, which prohibit certain forms of behavior for children under a specified age. An act which violates these specific prohibitions is a delinquent act. Thus, when a scientist identifies an act as delinquent, he merely indicates his awareness that the act deviates from the laws of the state. Such an identification in itself implies no personal evaluation of the act by the scientist, leaving him free to argue that the statutes are in error or to seek a change in the statutes, if he so desires.[7]

As is further noted in the following material, some of the behavioral patterns examined, while deviating from the delinquency statutes of New York State or from the more general nonlegal values and norms of the middle class, appear to be regarded as culturally normative, and in some cases, laudatory, when viewed by some of the residents of the ethnic neighborhood in which they occur.

And finally it must be noted that the process whereby a particular behavioral item or the normative pattern of a particular group is defined as deviant and opposed by another group is a highly important and sociologically relevant phenomenon. However, regardless of the nature of this process and of the scientist's judgment of it, it is still imperative to indicate that the behavioral item in question is judged to be deviant and is negatively sanctioned by a group which possesses the structural power to enforce its normative standards.

In sum, from the social point of view, "delinquency" is a relative term, and no adolescent is in any absolute sense a delinquent. The words "delinquency" and "delinquent" are labels applied to the behavior of some people by others who disapprove of it and who have the status, resources, and influence to make the labels stick.

Two other propositions must be mentioned at this point:

The first is that there is one effective strategy by which a community group can prevent many of its children who have been defined as "troublesome" from being processed officially as delinquents. This involves providing a diversionary extralegal system of care to deflect the children from the official law enforcement process into other social institutions, particularly private welfare. Writing of delinquency in New York City in 1930, Sophia Robison suggested that differences in the incidence of official delinquency at that time among different religious groups were strongly influenced by the type and number of other welfare services available. Thus, in the case of the Jewish group in Manhattan and the Bronx which had an active private welfare organization, the incidence of official delinquency was decidedly low, as compared with other religious groups.[8] Robison went on to point out that the type of care afforded delinquents varied widely according to race and religion, with institutional care as contrasted to field agency care, for example, most often applied in the cases of Negro and Catholic children. Among several of the variables influencing the choice of treatment afforded in the cases examined, Robison lists the availability of alternatives to institutionalization, particularly as offered to Jewish children, in contrast, for instance, to Catholic children. Commitment of Catholic children prevailed, in part, because institutionalization was a preferred Catholic social work technique.[9]

This flow of children's cases to private agencies operated by groups of the same religious affiliation as the children involved has been facilitated by New York State law, which, since the late nineteenth century, has enforced this general requirement "where practicable." [10]

Based on this experience and on that of subsequent years, it seems fair to conclude that a serious maldistribution of services exists with respect to the welfare care of children from the various ethnic and religious groups in New York City, with Protestant Negro children suffering the most severe discrimination.[11] Without doubt, the availability of sectarian agency referral resources, frequently offering services far superior to those in the public sector, works inequities into child welfare practices in the city. Some groups prosper because their children in trouble have easy access to these scarce resources; others suffer, not because their children are less worthy, but because the adults, as ethnic interest groups, have not created or expanded their own welfare services. That in New York such special interest services are often largely paid for out of public funds serves to emphasize the resourcefulness and power of the groups which have created such programs.

The second proposition is that many of the difficulties besetting American ghettos would never exist if their residents possessed the political power to protect and advance their own self-interests. This statement may be obvious to the urban planner, experienced politician, or observant private citizen. It may even sound slightly tautological. Nevertheless, as Wordsworth put it in *Rob Roy's Grave:*

> *The good old rule, . . . the simple plan,*
> *That they should take who have the power*
> *And they should keep who can.*

In the sections that follow it is essential that an understanding of the neighborhood under study be drawn from this perspective. The many variables involved in the increase in official delinquency in East Tremont—the neighborhood studied—cannot all, of course, be explained solely in political terms. Nevertheless, in East Tremont and in thousands of similar urban ghettos across the nation, political impotence is an important dimension of the crime and delinquency problems which are endemic to such areas. It is not simply that there is an absence of political power at the local level in East Tremont or in any other particular ghetto, but that ghetto dwellers lack established power at *every* political level: local, municipal, state, and national. It is not just that the Puerto Ricans and Negroes of East Tremont are powerless, but that they belong to ethnic and racial collectivities which wield scant institutionalized influence in most city halls, in most state capitals, and in Washington, D.C.

This aspect of the crime and delinquency question is now just beginning to emerge in public debate. As yet, it has had little effect on public policy. The President's Commission on Law Enforcement and Administration of Justice emphasized the present *unfairness* of the system of criminal justice. When it is realized that most of those processed by the criminal justice system are poor and very often from the urban ghettos, the full political significance and consequence of such unfairness begin to unfold. Combined with the personal, familial, cultural, and other variables in which delinquency is rooted in urban slums, the political perspective adds an essential dimension to a structural understanding of this behavior. More attention will be given this issue in the concluding chapter. For now it is perhaps sufficient to quote what Kenneth Clark said in 1965 about the prevailing lack of interest among both scholars and professionals up to that time in the problem of the powerlessness of the urban ghetto and how it feels to be a prisoner inside one:

> To my knowledge, there is at present nothing in the vast literature of social science treatises and textbooks and nothing in the practical or field training of graduate students in social science to prepare them for the realities and complexities of . . . involvement in a real, dynamic, turbulent, and at times seemingly chaotic community. And what is more, nothing anywhere in the training of social scientists, teachers, or social workers now prepares them to understand, to cope with, or to change the normal chaos of ghetto communities. These are grave lacks which must be remedied soon if these disciplines are to become relevant to the stability and survival of our society.[12]

Attention will now be directed to the Bronx neighborhood which was intensively studied in the research being reported.

Sources of Information About East Tremont

The East Tremont section was chosen, by means of the method of area analysis, as a suitable demonstration site for the Juvenile Court Community Development Project. This source of information about the area provided considerable data about the neighborhood, its history, and its changing character, as well as about its relationship to the changing New York community. Particular emphasis was placed upon the relationship of the area to the growth-and-change characteristic of the Bronx itself.

A second source of information about the demonstration neighborhood was provided by an intensive investigation of individual adolescent area residents who were under probationary supervision by the Bronx Branch of the New York City Office of Probation. The sociogenic case history method and the method of situational analysis, described in earlier chapters, were used in studying the youngsters examined. The sociogenic case history method provided an understanding of the social organization and cultural patterns characteristic of the demonstration neighborhood, as seen from the point of view of the adolescents studied. The situational analysis of their reported delinquent activities provided the cross-cultural definitions and contradictions in the description and explanation of these activities, which constitute a vital dimension in the structural analysis of delinquency.

Nine youngsters were intensively studied in this manner, each by a team of from four to six members, including sociologists, social workers, a psychiatrist or psychologist, and a social psychologist.* The youngsters examined were drawn from a total of twelve juveniles, living in the two core census tracts of the East Tremont area, who were on probation as delinquents or PINS in the Family Court on March 1, 1967. During 1965 and 1966, a total of eighty-five delinquents and PINS from the two core tracts were referred by the Family Court to the Office of Probation for social investigation. Referral was customary and automatic, once a case had been officially adjudicated by the court and the individual declared a delinquent or PINS. The nine adolescents studied were the total from the group of twelve on probation as of March 1, 1967 who could be located and inter-

---

* It should not be concluded from this team approach that, in carrying out the structural analysis of delinquency, individual youngsters must be studied by investigators working in such combinations. Once the basic area analysis of a neighborhood has been completed by a demographic team, it would seem that individual delinquents from the area might properly be examined, according to the new approach, by a social worker closely supported by a psychiatrist or psychologist, provided that both worker and clinician are properly trained in the new methodology.

viewed by the project staff responsible for carrying out this phase of the demonstration.

It is significant to note here that the major understanding of the internal structure of the East Tremont area was provided by the intensive study of only nine cases. Each case served as a point of entry into the area for the investigators, enabling them to probe beyond the limits of the type of information ordinarily made available to outsiders by the method of area analysis when used alone. This research technique is very similar to that used by cultural anthropologists when they employ key indigenous informants to provide detailed information about primitive societies. It is also very similar to the technique used by William Whyte when, through his informants "Doc" and "Chick," he was able to study the organization and culture of his Cornerville. Maurice Stein suggests that Whyte "provides a model of sociological reporting in this connection," as he continually moves between his informants' "personal characteristics, their life plans, and their peer associations, on the one hand, and their relations with the institutions of Cornerville, on the other." [13]

The depth and scope of the information revealed about the East Tremont section through the study of these nine cases suggests that: (1) the general method of structural analysis of delinquent behavior being presented yields considerable understanding about a high-delinquency area after a study of only a few of the total number of official cases resident in the area; and (2) there seems to be good probability that the routine study of a somewhat larger number of cases done in the same manner on a continuing basis each year would provide a most valuable understanding of an area under scrutiny in terms of its changing social and cultural characteristics and their relationship to local delinquency patterns.

A third source of information about the East Tremont area was provided by the Juvenile Court Project's field unit, which was active in the neighborhood for twenty months in the course of the two-year demonstration. This field unit consisted of a social work field supervisor and a secretary, operating out of a local apartment office during the project's first year. During the project's second year, the unit was expanded to include five students in social work community organization. During both years, the field operation was directed by one of the project's associate directors, who was a faculty member at the school of social work attended by the students.

This field unit furnished significant information valuable at the time of the initial selection of the project site, as described in the previous chapter. During the first year, the unit also served as a "pathfinding" operation for the second year of the demonstration by preparing the way for the student unit whose members were to work closely with various indigenous groups seeking to take collective action on neighborhood issues. In the course of its operations, the field unit became heavily involved and well-related both to local conditions and local people. In a very special sense, it became not only an "enabler" of local collective action, but also served as a close link between the project and the people in its demonstration site.

Late in January 1968, a working paper[14] was prepared by project staff, presenting an extended analysis of the East Tremont section, its delinquency patterns, and the structural roots of this behavior as revealed by the project's application of its assessment methodology. This working paper was then reviewed by the field unit's personnel for their judgments about its factual accuracy and conceptual validity. The field unit made several important modifications and qualifications of some of the factual material presented in it. In the main, however, the unit's review confirmed the general profile of the demonstration neighborhood, as drawn. This method of corroboration is similar to that used by Edwin Sutherland in his book, *The Professional Thief*, in which he asked other professional thieves, detectives, and so forth to judge the validity of the description of the profession of theft given to him by the thief with whom he worked.[15] This method does not provide positive proof about the validity of what was originally presented. It is particularly vulnerable in the matter of conceptualization and interpretation of the raw data used. However, it is probably no more subject to errors of validity and reliability than the customary methods used in psychoanalysis, social casework, cultural anthropology, political science, and related professions and academic disciplines—all of which seek first to describe and then to interpret the human condition.

The following section contains a summary assessment statement about the patterns of delinquency in the East Tremont neighborhood. It also relates these patterns to the massive structural changes which characterized the area during the period when delinquency became endemic in the neighborhood. The modifications in the original working paper about the demonstration site which were suggested by the project's field unit have been incorporated.

The Making of a Modern Ghetto

The demonstration neighborhood of the Juvenile Court Project shows in microcosm what can go wrong in American cities. The processes of urban blight at work in this section of the central Bronx have developed so quickly and spread with such intensity that they furnish, when properly documented, a clear case report of the forces that can lead into the making of a modern American ghetto. The task and challenge here is to present, as succinctly and accurately as possible, what happened to and within the East Tremont neighborhood and how such changes were related to the rise of endemic delinquency in the area.

In making the case for explaining delinquency in East Tremont as a consequence of structural change which is itself rooted in massive population shifts, it is necessary to relate, both logically and conceptually, the rise in delinquency in the neighborhood to the recent population shifts that occurred there.

This was the general goal which guided the whole study of delinquency being presented. The theory and methodology used are reported in the earlier chapters. Yet, even before research on the East Tremont section was begun and before that section of the Bronx had been selected as the demonstration site for the

Juvenile Court Community Development Project, there existed a vague, somewhat imprecise, understanding on the part of the principal researchers involved that questions of political power were also crucial in understanding delinquent behavior. Thus, for example, in their book, *Delinquent Behavior,*[16] John Martin and Joseph Fitzpatrick raised the question of power and its influence on theory, on public policy, and on programs in the delinquency field and the more general area of law enforcement.

Growing out of these beginnings, and heavily reinforced by a rapidly emerging national consciousness about the realities of power as it relates to the whole field of what is popularly called social problems, it seemed essential to the researchers that the power aspects and political dimensions of the delinquency question be addressed directly. The etiological question of why delinquent behavior occurs must be explored; but more must be done. Searching probes must be made to find out why some children and youths end up in court for their misbehavior, while others do not.

The principal thrust of what follows will be to provide a structural interpretation of why delinquency has become endemic in the East Tremont section in recent years. Essentially etiological, an effort will be made to illustrate in a concrete fashion what can be seen when one uses a structural approach in trying to understand delinquency in a modern ghetto.

Something else will also be attempted. Within the limitations of the data at hand, which are considerable, an effort will be made to begin to document the relationship of the presence or absence of power to delinquency prevention and control in a given neighborhood. Since delinquency, which is generally rather broadly defined, seems to be a universal behavior pattern in which all children and youths are involved at some time or other,[17] a critical question emerges as to why some adolescents are acted upon officially for what they do, while others are not. The critical question here is that of *official action,* and not that of the etiology of delinquent behavior. Tentative efforts have been made to examine why some official decision makers, such as policemen, route some adolescents into the system of criminal justice, while other adolescents, who often commit the same illegal acts, are screened out.[18] The differentiating variables often seem to rest upon what might be called the life styles of the individual adolescents involved—that is, the way in which each youth and his family live—and how given policemen react to and judge what they see when they look at such cases. A variable very much involved in the decision-making process at this point appears to be the demeanor or attitude of the youth toward the police officer, with "fresh punks," to use the police idiom, usually getting arrested. More recent research has suggested that the very "professionalism" of given police departments may significantly influence adolescent arrest rates.[19] Thus the police seem more likely to handle juvenile cases formally, as opposed to informally, if their professional standards, such as formal educational prerequisites and on-the-job supervision, are high and if more emphasis is put on centralized, insulated, juvenile bureaus, as distinct from juvenile officers operating at the local precinct level in close association with ordinary patrolmen. On the whole, however, very little information exists about the decision-making process in the system of criminal justice as it relates to offenders, whether juveniles or adults. Almost all of the research in crime and delinquency has focused on the characteristics of offenders and the offenses they commit and not upon the decision-making process and the characteristics of decision makers themselves in the field of criminal justice. Nevertheless, a strong suspicion exists—and in some camps it may even be an operating principle—that the poor, especially poor members of colored minority groups, get the worst deal. In keeping with the temper of the times, it is a good hunch that poor black militants who get in trouble with the law are likely to have an especially difficult time of it, unless a countervailing policy in criminal justice is developed and successfully implemented at the individual case decision-making level.

To date, almost no attention whatsoever has been given to still another aspect of criminal justice: How have different interest groups, operating from within given neighborhood frameworks or outside of them, organized themselves to protect their adolescents from being defined as "troublesome" by officials and, once so defined, from being formally routed as cases to be processed by the criminal justice system? It seems likely that to avoid the negative consequences of official action, various ethnic, religious, and other special interest groups have in fact created institutional arrangements which serve, wherever possible, to divert their youth out of the system of criminal justice.

If this problem is approached on a different tack—by asking how communities can better organize to prevent their children and youth from getting into trouble, in the first instance, as well as for meeting other kinds of local problems—much more information and insight from the fields of community development and planning can be brought to bear in framing an answer.[20] But even here, as in many other areas of collective life, much more is unknown than known.

When it comes to comparing how different types of local communities have organized or failed to organize to meet the challenge of delinquency and other youth problems, very little information of any sort seems to exist. The experience of the Juvenile Court Community Development Project in the central Bronx provides an opportunity to begin to lay down the main lines of one such comparative study. Two communities, a stone's throw from each other in the central Bronx, are almost ideally suited for such a comparative analysis. They are the communities of East Tremont and Belmont. East Tremont has lived through dramatic changes since the early 1960s, including a sharp and rapid increase in official delinquency. Belmont, a tightly knit Italian neighborhood lying immediately north of East Tremont, has experienced much less change in recent years, and very few of its many adolescents have been involved in official delinquency. Figure 8 shows both communities and gives their boundaries in census tract terms.

Most of the following material in this chapter will provide a summary assessment of what the Juvenile Court Project staff was able to learn about delinquency and its structural roots in the East Tremont community through the application of the project's assessment process. The research base from which this

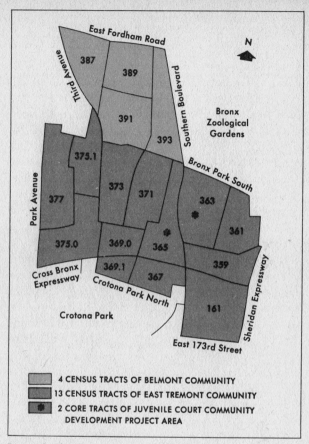

Figure 8. The East Tremont and Belmont Sections of the Bronx, New York City, 1968

description was obtained organized information about the area and the people living in it around several principal themes: the rapid demographic transition characteristic of the area; the major "institutional dislocations" found in the area; the social and psychological isolation of the area's youth; and the presence of cultural supports for delinquency and other forms of deviation from middle-class norms found among the people in the area. After East Tremont has been described, the final sections of this chapter will also present, within the limits of existing data, the Belmont case, and a closing summary statement will be made about the relationship between the two communities. Particular attention will also be paid to what seems to be significantly different about the two communities in terms of their capacities to take care of the needs of their youth. The objective of this inquiry is not to determine, for example, whether Italian-Americans are in any basic way "better" than Puerto Rican and black Americans. Today most social and behavioral scientists would agree that it is absurd to believe that the many differences which exist between Belmont and East Tremont, or any two communities for that matter, are attributable to differences in biology.[21] They would also agree that many of the noticeable differences between communities reflect differences in culture, and in the social capacities of the residents to develop their resources and their ties with outside constituencies and coalitions, and to take and hold what they need. This sort of interpretation is also likely to prevail among many citizens without special expertise in social and behavioral science, especially if they themselves either live in similar communities or identify with those who do.

Summary Assessment of the East Tremont Community

A great deal of sociology emphasizes the significance of institutional structures in maintaining a social order and the necessity for a logical and viable relationship between the values and norms of a society and the institutional structures through which these norms and values are articulated and realized. Conformity to cultural expectations—including those set down in the laws of the state—is strengthened when the people of the community are linked positively to institutional structures which support these norms and values. It is, then, a common sociological principle that the degree of conformity to legal prohibitions against traditional forms of crime and delinquency in a given community is positively correlated with the strength of the "fit" between the people in a community and the conventional institutions operating there. In American society, these institutional complexes would include the schools, the churches, the family, the world of work, as well as agencies of criminal justice and other public and private organizations designed to enhance the general welfare. In well-organized communities, all these institutions exhibit and enforce normative prohibitions against most forms of delinquency. When these institutions are not efficiently related to the children and youth in a given community, the sociologist would expect to find a relatively high degree of delinquency. When there is a lack of good fit between almost all the extrafamilial institutions in a local community and the people— both adults and juveniles—living in that community, crime, delinquency, and other conspicuous forms of social deviancy, as measured by outside standards, should be rampant. Underlying such visible measures of deviation, the sociologist might also expect to find the following: considerable culture conflict between outsiders and their representatives and the people living in the local area; feelings of alienation, suspicion, and hostility between outsiders and insiders; and, from the point of view of a conflict theorist viewing an urban ghetto, a paucity of formally organized local groups which are capable of mediating between local residents and a basically indifferent, and in many ways hostile, wider society.

This seems to describe with some precision the situation in East Tremont in the mid-1960s.

The best place to start to understand East Tremont, it would seem, is with a brief review of the massive ethnic shifts which have occurred in the Bronx in recent years. These changes have been particularly significant in what has been identified as the south-central Bronx rectangle, where delinquency in the borough is concentrated. The East Tremont demonstration site was located in the northern sector of this rectangle. Here the population shifts involved a rapid change from lower-middle-class white to lower-class Puerto Rican and Negro. Some measure of the extent and rapidity of these changes is provided by the public school and birth statistics for the area reviewed in the previous chapter. The school statistics are particularly instructive. Five of the eight elementary and junior high schools in the area experienced more than a 65 per cent increase in enrollment between 1957 and 1965. Six of the eight were reported as operating at over 111 per cent* of capacity in 1965. Finally, while whites, who were not Puerto Rican, comprised 60 per cent or more of the students in all but one of these schools in 1957, by 1965 they were a small minority in all of them. In only one school did the white children comprise over 20 per cent of the student population, while in five of the eight schools they accounted for less than 15 per cent.

The total population of the East Tremont demonstration neighborhood (represented in Figure 4, see Chapter 3) was 80,556 in 1960. Of this total, 82 per cent were white, and about 10.5 per cent Puerto Rican and 7.5 per cent Negro. Thus, as late as 1960, there were markedly fewer Puerto Ricans and Negroes in the area than were present in the Bronx as a whole, whose population that year included 13.1 per cent Puerto Rican and 11.5 per cent Negro. Certainly there were fewer Puerto Ricans and Negroes in the area in 1960 than in other areas lying to the south within the boundaries of the south-central Bronx rectangle.

Examination of census data for the period 1920–1960 reveals that the East Tremont neighborhood reached a peak population of close to 100,000 in the period between 1930 and 1940, ten or more years in advance of the total Bronx, which peaked at 1,451,277 in 1950. Moreover, census data for the East Tremont section since 1930 indicate that, even as late as 1950, the community was over 98 per cent white in its ethnic composition. In contrast, by 1950 the population in the total Bronx had become slightly less than 90 per cent white.

These data suggest that the East Tremont community reached a peak population ahead of the total Bronx; remained

---

* Normal capacity is defined by the New York City Board of Education as between 90 and 110 per cent of a school's capacity.

white for a longer period than did the total Bronx, particularly when compared with other areas lying immediately to the south; and, as suggested by school and birth statistics, rapidly became a heavily Puerto Rican and Negro area during the first half of the 1960s. Unfortunately, unless a special census of the area is done prior to the regular 1970 census, no hard data about the size of the total population in the area and its ethnic, economic, and other characteristics will be available until the new census figures are reported.

In sum, large-scale ethnic changes accompanied by a rapid increase in the child population occurred in the East Tremont project site during the first half of the 1960s. In this same period, there was a marked rise in the number of delinquency cases in the area as measured by the type of Family Court data presented in the previous chapter—that is, adjudicated delinquents and PINS referred to the Office of Probation for social investigation. Using this measure, as previously reported, the two core census tracts of the demonstration neighborhood experienced the largest increase of any of the high-delinquency areas in the Bronx which were studied. Between 1963, when the two tracts had 15 cases, and 1965, when they had 48, the increase was well over 200 per cent. The increase for the total thirteen tracts in the project site for the same periods, although not as large, was also considerable: in 1963 the total case count was 71; in 1965 it was 114—an increase of approximately 60 per cent.

Police crime statistics released to the public for the first time in 1968[22] confirm the extent of known offenses in the area: for the ten-month period, January through October 1967, the 48th Police Precinct in which the East Tremont section is situated was the second highest in total crimes of the eleven precincts in the Bronx; the highest of the Bronx precincts was the 41st, immediately adjacent to the 48th to the south and east, while the third highest was the 42nd, immediately adjacent to the 48th to the south. On a city-wide basis, the 48th was the eighth highest of a total of seventy-nine precincts.

Information provided by the commanding officer of the 48th Precinct confirmed that he and other police officers defined the East Tremont section, especially that part around or within the two core census tracts of the Juvenile Court Community Development Project, as previously described, to be a very active and difficult area from a policeman's point of view. These officers further reported that the section used to be relatively quiet, with most of the police activity in the 48th concentrated farther south. However, by late 1967, the northern part of the precinct, wherein the Juvenile Court Project was conducted, had become increasingly difficult.

Nonstatistical assessment data available about East Tremont reveal qualitative information about delinquency patterns endemic in the area. Interviews with known delinquents, with their families and friends, and with other adults in the area indicated that the use and sale of marijuana was widespread, so prevalent that the drug may be described as a "focal concern" [23] among youth in the area at the time the assessment was made. Local adolescents readily admitted having used the drug, saw nothing wrong with such behavior, and were quite knowledgeable and articulate about the different grades of marijuana, the best methods for using it, the prices to pay for it, the prices to charge when selling it, as well as where to buy and sell it locally. Although the information was less firm, a number of adult informants insisted that heroin, as well as marijuana, was in the area, and many were very angry about the presence of these drugs. The youths interviewed all denied any contact with heroin and condemned those who might use it, although they too acknowledged it was in the area. The existence of heroin in the community was also confirmed by some of the police officers interviewed.

Stealing from local stores and breaking and entering into warehouses situated slightly to the east of East Tremont was also common among local youth. Much of what was stolen appeared to be sold to other local merchants who, in turn, sold it again to other customers.

Car theft and joyriding were also quite common practices in the community. Sometimes the cars were stolen and stripped, with the parts being sold off to local gas stations and mechanics, and sometimes they were just driven around for fun and excitement.

Thus a firm pattern of theft seemed well established among youth in the area. This pattern was supported, in part, by what appeared to be a practice among some local adults of trafficking in stolen goods. Other adults interviewed seemed perplexed and troubled by this predatory pattern, expressed their bitterness over this aspect of the more general change that had come over the neighborhood, but could find no effective way of doing anything about what was happening.

The evidence was also very strong in the assessment data that a pattern of early sexual intercourse among young adolescents was common in the area. The boys and girls interviewed who participated in such behavior did not consider it wrong. They certainly did not look upon it as illegal. And a number of the adults and parents interviewed tolerated the behavior, although others expressed their concern, especially when pregnancies resulted. In several of the families from the area which were examined intensively, sexual intercourse among boys and girls thirteen and fourteen years of age was a common phenomenon, rooted in cultural practices which, over the generations, went back to the ties the families had to the rural South or to Puerto Rico.

Truancy and dropping out of school were also endemic in the area. Several of the youths examined intensively belonged to fairly large peer groups in which most of the members were both out of school and out of work. Some of these youths, who were Puerto Rican, got into trouble with authorities when their parents, usually their mothers, complained to authorities about the late hours their sons were keeping while out with their friends in the local poolrooms and other hangouts.

By late 1967 and early 1968, a number of Negro youths in the area were becoming increasingly active in the black nationalist movement. Although this behavior cannot be viewed as strictly illegal, it is reported because of the concern outsiders to urban ghettos frequently show about such involvement. Moreover, many of the Negro and Puerto Rican adults interviewed also expressed their concern about the development of this activity in their community. There is some suggestion in the data that some local Negro youths had first been attracted to black nationalism while in a youth detention facility for the Family Court, that ties existed between local youth in the movement and Harlem, and that participants in the movement seemed much more numerous in sections lying farther south of East Tremont, more toward the center of what has been described as the south-central Bronx rectangle.

The assessment data indicated a very strong and conscious realization of neighborhood boundaries on the part of East Tremont youth. Almost all interviewed agreed that 181st or 182nd Street would be the northern boundary beyond which they would not venture without a large number of friends. The Belmont community begins at this point. The characteristics of this Italian community, and its relationships with the East Tremont section, will be presented in a later section. It suffices at this point to note that there was sustained, on-going conflict between the two areas; that the youth in East Tremont were quite conscious of this conflict; and that they readily recalled incidents in which this strife had erupted into violence, which usually occurred when boys from East Tremont ventured north into the Italian section. The Italians did not often come down into East Tremont. The conflict was aggravated by the fact that a number of young people from the East Tremont area attended public schools either in or near the Italian section.

Much of the assessment data indicate rather conclusively that many adolescents and adults in the East Tremont area were angry about, hostile toward, or simply indifferent to various local institutions. Not one of the youths interviewed had a good word to say about his school. They were all failing academically and were inclined to see school as terribly boring, with subjects that made no sense to them. Even boys with high I.Q.s among those examined had consistent records of school failure. General reading achievement scores for the various public schools in the area were considerably below normal for the 1965–1966 academic year, and the disparity between the normal level expected and the real level achieved *increased* as the grade level went up.[24] Parents were also embittered about the quality of education being offered in their community. Even the teachers themselves were angry, frustrated, and vigorously protesting the state of public education in the community. During 1967, several local teachers' groups picketed in public protest about their working conditions, and mothers' groups were equally vocal about their displeasure with local education. Sometimes both teachers and mothers picketed together.

The same sort of estrangement was found to exist between local residents and other institutions, particularly the police, the Family Court, and the Office of Probation serving juveniles in the area. This hostility did not erupt into demonstrations. Instead it would break out in local meetings or work its way into conversations and interviews with the staff of the Juvenile Court Project. One principal theme kept recurring, however: many local residents, both adults and juveniles, were grossly unhappy about the relationships they personally had had with the police, Family Court, and Office of Probation. Other residents were quite critical of the police in a general way for what they called the "inadequate protection" afforded their community. One of the most startling discoveries was that probation officers serving the community knew very little about the area itself in terms of the specifics of its social and cultural characteristics or about the on-going life experiences of neighborhood adolescents, even the ones they were supervising. The written case material prepared about area delinquents by probation officers contained hardly any references to the characteristics of the neighborhood itself or the relationship of each youth examined to his peers and to other aspects of his milieu. Aware of this critical knowledge gap, the directors of the Office of Probation were, by late 1967, attempting to decentralize their services and otherwise put their workers into closer contact with their clients and their clients' subcommunities.

The churches in East Tremont also appeared to be remote from the lives of the delinquents examined intensively and from the lives of their families and many friends. Usually the people were simply not affiliated with any church, and that was that. The very paucity of data which the assessment process was able to uncover on concrete relationships between local people interviewed and the churches which were obviously physically present in the neighborhood is suggestive of the insignificant role played by these institutions in the lives of many of the people most in need in East Tremont. On the other hand, it began to appear in late 1967 and early 1968 that several of the Protestant churches were making serious efforts to become involved in East Tremont on the level of local issues through efforts to participate in and stimulate "grassroots" community action groups.

As of spring 1968, one of the most outstanding institutional deficits of the East Tremont community was the lack of any one organization or interest group which could effectively speak for the people of the area and mediate and interpret their needs to the broader community. Nor was there present in the area an effective grassroots organization to provide a structure around and through which residents might act collectively to state clearly the blighted condition of their existence as a first step toward getting what they need and must have to survive. The strongest institution situated in the community, the local YMHA, around which much of the required indigenous organization might have been achieved, closed down in June 1968 as a consequence of the flight of the East Tremont Jewish population.

In March 1967 the New York City Board of Estimate officially appropriated $456,500 of antipoverty funds for what was called the "East Tremont" community. The area designated to receive the funds included all the territory covered by the Juvenile Court Community Development Project and half of the neighboring Belmont community. In order to receive the money, the designated area had to form a Community Corporation. The municipal Community Development Agency conducted local elections during the spring and summer of 1967 to start an East Tremont Planning Committee which was to set the guidelines for establishing the Community Corporation and the election of its board. When this is finally accomplished, the corporation will establish policy with respect to the local use of the allocated anti-poverty money. The formation of the Planning Committee was delayed, however, until January 1968 because some of the results of the election which established the committee were contested. The committee finally started work very early in 1968 with a reduced budget of $220,000. By March of that year, this amount had been further drastically reduced because of federal economies. As of that time, the Community Corporation itself had yet to be formed. It remains to be seen whether antipoverty money will facilitate the effective organization for collective action of the people of East Tremont or whether, as so often happens, it will only lead to deepened antagonisms, particularly between local Puerto Ricans and Negroes.

This, then, was the East Tremont community as it appeared to the staff of the Juvenile Court Project which operated in the area. A number of summary conclusions about the area, its people, and its problems may now be presented.

The change in ethnic and racial composition of the area has quite probably resulted in a decline in the neighborhood's age structure. If the increased school enrollment statistics and the age structure of most other Puerto Rican and Negro neighborhoods in the city have any bearing on East Tremont, it should be expected that the number of children under sixteen has increased considerably. Awareness of this phenomenon, when viewed along with the conditions of deprivation typical of minority-group life in the urban North, is probably crucial for understanding the increase in delinquency in the area.

Perhaps even more important than demographic transition itself are the multitude of structural problems and changes that often follow. Foremost among these is the likelihood that the population changes will upset the normal functioning of the area's social institutions. In a well-structured community, the values and norms of these local institutions will reflect and be responsive to the needs and cultural traditions of the people they are designed to serve. When this condition of corresponding similarity exists, the institutions will probably be accessible to the people and prove to be effective channels through which the people can realize their shared aspirations. Since the expectations of these institutions are in keeping with the cultural traditions of the people, the people are likely to identify with and otherwise relate cooperatively to those institutions.

An effective pattern of response between people and their local institutions is apt to be seriously threatened when the population undergoes profound and rapid change. The needs which the institutions previously served may be replaced by new needs. The cultural context within which the institutions developed may be replaced by a new cultural climate—one that is less compatible with established institutionalized expectations. Because of the bureaucratic formality which characterizes the organization of institutions in American society, these structures are not likely to adapt themselves at a pace approximating that with which the population has changed. In such circumstances, what may be called institutional dislocations[25] emerge.

The institutions are not quick to recognize the peculiar needs of the new population. But even when these needs are recognized, the political climate of the larger community makes the institutions hesitant about accepting the needs as legitimate. As a result, the institutions prove to be less accessible and less responsive to the people and to provide less effective channels through which the latter may realize their aspirations.

For their part, the new residents find themselves on the outside of the conventional institutional structure. There is a consequent tendency to deny the relevance or even the legitimacy of these institutions. The new people lack a vested interest in sustaining them, and consequently, the support which effective conventional institutions lend to conventional norms and values is weakened.

Henry McKay makes a related and most significant comment about this same structural question in a brief note he recently published about changing neighborhoods and delinquency in Chicago.[26] He dismisses the notion that increasing delinquency rates in some of the neighborhoods in that city reflect the greater criminality inherent in incoming ethnic groups. Instead, he suggests that delinquency increases in rapidly changing neighborhoods where basic institutional roles have been disrupted. Thus, in the Chicago neighborhoods he studied, which were the areas of greatest change, he found that delinquency rates increased where white middle-class populations were replaced by Negroes, but that there were significant *decreases* in long-established Negro areas where the population had had several decades to make an adjustment to urban life. He also suggests that the present Negro areas with increasing delinquency rates may be very similar to the Negro areas with presently decreasing rates, as they were thirty or more years ago.

Much of the data presented about the East Tremont area suggest that the neighborhood is now struggling with the problems of institutional dislocations or what McKay calls "disruption of institutional roles." The police, courts, correctional agencies, schools, religious organizations, and so on—which in the area previously related to a stable, lower-middle-class population—appear to be inadequately sensitive to or in sympathy with the needs of the more deprived newcomers in the area. In some instances, as with the schools, the institutions seem to be overwhelmed. The people respond in kind. They manifest an indifference to and alienation from the conventional institutional structures. If the suspicion that the area is characterized by a high youth unemployment rate is correct, this same gap exists between the people in the East Tremont area and the American business establishment. The local institutions have failed to adapt to the needs and cultural traditions of the new minority poor in the community, although there appear to be a relatively large number of city-wide social agencies servicing the area. In some cases, the goals of these organizations, such as the building of a Community Corporation to unite the people and to facilitate the spending of antipoverty funds in the area, may not meet realistically the ethnic and racial rivalries already at work in the area or likely to be stimulated by the arrival of antipoverty money. And finally, other agencies, including the Family Court and the Office of Probation, are defined by their youthful clientele in the area as punitive and regulatory agencies rather than as agencies rendering concrete assistance and help.

Although a number of adults in the community were both aware of and concerned about the deteriorating state of their neighborhood, most of them could not see how the trend might be reversed. Many of these adults, who were themselves Negroes and Puerto Ricans, believed that one important reason for the demise of the area was the mass exodus of the white people. And they may well be right. Since the Negroes and Puerto Ricans did not see the return of the whites as being very probable, none expressed optimism about the future of the East Tremont area.

This lack of an effective, integrated institutional structure in the East Tremont area is compounded by the existence of sustained tension and conflict between the people of the area and the Italian residents of the neighboring Belmont community. To a lesser extent, similar conflict seems to exist with other whites living east. The only open border seems to be the southern one, which simply faces the vast ghettos lying off in that direction. To the north, the conflict is drawn tightly, with the Italians especially manifesting vigorous and sometimes violent opposition to any northerly movement on the part of the Puerto Ricans and Negroes out of East Tremont.

Under certain circumstances, such external conflict may contribute to the internal cohesion of a community. However, it is doubtful that this conflict will have such an effect upon East Tremont. At present, this area is faced with a broad range of "social problems" which cannot be effectively addressed, partly because the community lacks an effective, well-organized internal structure. In the absence of such a structure, attempts to deal with external conflict are likely to be diffuse and uncoordinated. Conflict resolution may tend to be episodic and defensive rather than purposefully organized toward the achievement of clearly defined strategic goals.

Related to, but distinct from, the general institutional dislocations existing in the East Tremont area, is the apparent isolation of youth from the world of adults. The dislocations discussed above are likely to be reflected in the alienation of youth from conventional institutions. The data about the East Tremont area—to wit, the prevalence of delinquent behavior patterns, the apparent large number of neighborhood youth who are both unemployed and out of school, the high degree of reading deficiency among those attending school, and the widespread tendency for the youth to define negatively representatives of conventional institutions—all further suggest that these institutions are marginal to the life of the community.

What is distinctive here, however, is the data's suggestion that the youth of the East Tremont area are not only alienated from external institutional representatives but are also apparently isolated from the adult world of their own community. The adolescents studied intensively had little positive contact with adult role models, even within their own families. These young people spent very little time at home. For the most part, they played and lived together—in the streets, poolrooms, and other hangouts dotting the neighborhood. In many cases, they were not even economically dependent upon their families, becoming quite accustomed to fending for themselves by means of a variety of predatory activities. Their world seemed virtually isolated against adult penetration.

The problems of culture conflict are fairly obvious for the Puerto Rican youth. He is caught between the cultural expectations of an urban American society and those of a Puerto Rican society from which his parents have often migrated. In these circumstances, his parents are likely to prove ineffective role models. The youth does not see their way of life, their experiences, as relevant to his life in New York City. Neither the institutional structures of the large society nor the advice of his parents is particularly helpful, and the foundation is laid for the emergence of his peers as an exclusive reference group.

The typical Negro youth examined had parents who were products of a rural southern experience. Similar problems of culture conflict were characteristic of these families. In general, the adults in the life of the Negro youth are themselves in the throes of adjusting to life in the urban North. Furthermore, Negroes, both young and old, are attempting this adjustment at a time when a new and more militant concept of collective identity is emerging among young Negroes. This new concept is in part a reaction against what the younger generation of American Negroes perceive to be the passivity and collective inferiority complex of their ancestors in America. The fact that the issue is often drawn in terms of specific age-grade cleavages is likely to contribute to the Negro youth's sense of isolation from Negro adults. The fact that some form of black nationalist ideology is beginning to influence Negro youths in the East Tremont area may provide some insight into some of the consequences of the isolation of youth in that community.

Living in their own world, largely detached from both conventional institutions and the indigenous adult population, many of the youth in East Tremont appear to have developed certain concerns of their own. These include the use and sale of marijuana, racial and ethnic conflict, petty theft, and early sexual experience—all of which receive reference group support. The prevalence of these delinquency patterns and the social reward system that is apparently attached to them lead to the conclusion that the East Tremont area is characterized by strong cultural and organizational supports for delinquent behavior. In some instances, such support is provided only by peers; but at times, it is provided by both peers and adults.

In sum, the data suggest that delinquency in the East Tremont area is to be understood in terms of the relationship among four variables: (1) profound demographic transition; (2) serious institutional dislocations; (3) marked social and psychological isolation of the youth from the world of adults; and (4) widespread cultural supports for various forms of delinquent behavior and other forms of deviation from middle-class norms. An appreciation of the East Tremont area in terms of this field of forces provides the context within which the individual youth from the area coming before the police, the courts, and the correctional agencies can best be understood. This context reveals the key environmental components underlying his delinquent behavior, which itself can then be understood in terms of the *motivational-situational-cultural complexes* within which it occurs. Finally, this total view of East Tremont reveals the present incapacity of the people there to act collectively and decisively, as a first, but significant, step toward getting what they want.

Brief Description of the Belmont Community*

In stark contrast to East Tremont is the Belmont community. Belmont has been essentially Italian and substantially working class since before World War I. It grew out of an earlier, disadvantaged, immigrant community. It made it by becoming a highly organized, politically and economically powerful, urban enclave. Yet, at the same time, Belmont has also been dedicated to maintaining its ethnic identity in the heart of a rapidly changing borough. This becomes a most difficult and perhaps impossible task to accomplish, since Belmont is situated right at the northern edge of the south-central Bronx rectangle. Faced by the massive population shifts flowing up the rectangle out of the south Bronx, Belmont, during the past several years, has already started to change. Large numbers of Puerto Ricans and Negroes are now found in Belmont's public schools and playgrounds, and some are occasionally seen eating in its restaurants and living in a few of its apartments here and there. But it

* This neighborhood was not studied as part of the original design of the Juvenile Court Community Development Project. The description presented here was obtained from various sources available from and through Fordham University, whose Bronx campus is situated directly across the street from Belmont, to the north. Particularly helpful in describing the area were sociology and political science student term papers and projects about the area; local informants from the area who had graduated from, or were presently attending, Fordham; and faculty members interested in urban studies who, through the years, had grown especially familiar with the area. Standard statistical sources were also used.

is also equally true that physical violence, usually undertaken by small groups of neighborhood youths, has long followed the movement of Negroes and Puerto Ricans into the area. Not all adults living in the neighborhood condone such behavior, and serious measures by community leaders have continuously been taken to curtail this violence. Nevertheless, the pattern of street violence has characterized the Belmont section for years, as racial tension has mounted. Despite the emphasis Belmont leaders place on curbing racial violence, these same leaders have acted in many complex and sophisticated ways to keep Belmont for the Italians. As one Belmont church leader put it publicly in April 1967, "This is all Italian in this area. We're not the kind who move. . . . Italians don't move!" [27] Less than a year later, a casual walk through the neighborhood suggests that what may have been true in 1967 is far less true in 1968. Belmont is no longer "all Italian." The Italians of Belmont do move, both politically and geographically. They negotiate and accommodate with newcomers over the use of local facilities; and some of them, at least, move their families and households right out of the area. In fact, for some time, many, especially younger adults, have been moving northward into other sections of the Bronx, into Westchester County, and across the Hudson River to New Jersey.

Belmont reached its maximum population of 31,533 in 1940, ten years ahead of the Bronx as a whole. While the absolute number of people in the Bronx has stayed relatively stable since 1940, the population of Belmont declined more than 20 per cent between 1940 and 1960. The decline was most severe in the ten years between 1950 and 1960, when it fell from 28,744 to 24,386—a drop of about 15 per cent. Thus, while Belmont has remained essentially white (it was 99 per cent white in 1950 and 97 per cent white in 1960) and Italian, its total population has sharply dropped from the peak reached in 1940. And observation of the eastern, southern, and western boundaries of the area indicates that on these fringes for several years Puerto Ricans and Negroes have been moving in large numbers into the apartments and shops vacated by the outgoing

Italians. Both groups of newcomers are heavily represented in the populations of the four public schools situated in Belmont.

Some measure of the power and influence of this Italian community is found in a comparison of the public schools in the area with those in the East Tremont community immediately to the south. Besides two public high schools, which serve a regional student population, two other public schools are situated in Belmont: P.S. 32 (elementary grades) and J.H.S. 45. In 1967 both were operating with a normal number of students— that is, somewhere between 90 and 110 per cent of capacity. In contrast, despite open protests to the Board of Education by both parents and teachers, most of the public schools in East Tremont were seriously overcrowded in 1967.

In the same year, P.S. 32 and J.H.S. 45, which draw their students from Belmont and surrounding sections, had student populations which were predominantly white. On the other hand, in the East Tremont schools, whites constituted only a small fraction of the student population in every school.

To keep the enrollment of its public elementary and junior high schools within normal limits, Belmont has the help of Our Lady of Mt. Carmel School. Built by the Italian community, Mt. Carmel is one of the largest and newest Catholic grammar schools in the Bronx. It has eight grades for boys and girls and a special preparatory ninth grade for those who seek extra help in an effort to enter Catholic high schools. In 1967 Our Lady of Mt. Carmel School enrolled 1,563 youngsters, of whom 96 per cent were white and largely Italian by ethnic origin. Many Belmont families want their children to attend Mt. Carmel. About two thirds of those who graduate from Mt. Carmel go on to academic study in Catholic high schools. Those who fail to make the grade at Mt. Carmel attend the local public schools: P.S. 32, which had an enrollment of 1,191 in 1967, and J.H.S. 45, which had an enrollment of 1,522 in the same year. From these two schools, local Italian youngsters go on to public high schools, including the two situated in Belmont. One of these, Theodore Roosevelt High School, on the northern edge of Belmont on Fordham Road, has increasingly become a center of racial tension and violence as whites, especially Italians from Belmont, confront Negroes and Puerto Ricans within what many Belmont Italians consider to be their sanctuary.

Most local informants agree that the Mt. Carmel School, with its close operating relationships with Catholic high schools, including the Fordham Preparatory School on the Fordham campus just across the street from Belmont, is one of the principal social institutions in the Belmont area. It is a good example of a local community institution which links a neighborhood with the institutions of the larger society. It eases its graduates onto the college-bound track and into the white-collar world of work. The educational process involved is a two-step one: from Mt. Carmel to a Catholic high school in the city and then, in many cases, from the Catholic high school to a Catholic college, such as Fordham or Manhattan. Belmont youngsters who do not follow this route often appear to end up on a different educational and career track. They usually attend public high school, often Roosevelt. Later their community facilitates their entrance into blue-collar work, such as construction, in which numerous New York Italians exercise considerable control. Entrance into this field is relatively easy for a Belmont youth. A large part of the Belmont labor force is already employed in construction work—about 12 per cent in 1960, as compared with only about 4 per cent of the total Bronx labor force that year.

As is often the case in Catholic parishes, Belmont youths who attend Mt. Carmel probably have more local prestige than youths in the public schools. They are also less often involved in any open racial hostility and violence. Much of the racial tension and violence between Italians and Puerto Ricans and Negroes in the area appears to revolve around the use of Roosevelt High School and J.H.S. 45. Moreover, it seems very clear that those in charge of the Mt. Carmel School will not long tolerate students who engage in any conspicuous racial hostility or violence. Despite this and other measures, however, the more established Belmont community seems unable to prevent periodic eruptions against "invading" Puerto Ricans and Negroes by many of its more violent youths.

There is not enough information available to determine if those Belmont youths who attend public schools or those who engage in racial fights and disturbances are, in social class or subcultural terms, different from those who do not. Nor is there enough information to describe in any detail the overall delinquency patterns characteristic of the area. However, one thing is perfectly clear. Very few Belmont youths find their way to the Bronx Family Court as delinquents or PINS for anything they do. For three of the years for which data are available (1963, 1965, and 1966), Belmont had a total of sixteen adolescents adjudicated as delinquents or PINS in the Family Court, compared with the hundred for the same years which were adjudicated from the two core census tracts of the Juvenile Court Project. During the same three years, the entire thirteen tracts of the Project's demonstration area in East Tremont generated three hundred cases. However, the few cases in the Belmont area have recently begun to increase: in 1966 there were six cases; in 1967, thirteen, whereas, in the two core tracts of the demonstration area, the numbers remained about the same: in 1966 there were thirty-seven cases; in 1967, thirty-eight.

The Mt. Carmel School, in effect, is but an arm of the Italian Catholic Parish, whose church, also called Our Lady of Mt. Carmel, is the hub of community life in Belmont and, in many respects, for a large number of Italians throughout the Bronx. Our Lady of Mt. Carmel Church is much more than just the large physical structure standing on East 187th Street. As has so frequently occurred in the Italian immigrant experience, the church has been the heart of the immigrant community. Consequently, Our Lady of Mt. Carmel is likewise much more than a religious institution. It is also a social and political organization composed of parish clergymen, parishioners in Belmont and elsewhere in the Bronx, with strong ties to municipal, state, and federal officials, to Italy, and to the Catholic Archdiocese of New York. The church's constituency also closely links it to banks, local real estate owners and businessmen, outside educational institutions, the construction trades and labor unions, various civic associations and local welfare services, both the

Democratic and Republican parties, and, some suspect, to the rackets.

Some measure of this church's influence and political skill, in the area of meeting local youth needs, is provided by the history of how the Madison Square Boys' Club came to Belmont in 1965 with a brand-new building and a predominantly Italian youth program. However, in the two or three years since its opening, the Belmont Boys' Club has undergone continuing ethnic change. The rapidity of this change reflects, it would seem, the massive population shifts occurring in the central Bronx, from which Belmont cannot remain isolated. It also reflects the ability of Belmont Italians to accommodate to the inevitable.

In 1964 a group of Belmont veterans who had been running an athletic open house at Roosevelt High School proposed that a full-time athletic facility be opened. The Madison Square organization expressed an interest, but many people in Belmont objected. The old men who used the proposed site as a garden objected; others argued that, with the Roosevelt High gym, the gym at J.H.S. 45, the gym at Mt. Carmel School, the Belmont Community Center, the Caiati Hall Youth Center near Mt. Carmel Church, the Police Athletic League program, the numerous well-equipped city parks, playgrounds, play streets, and other facilities, a new Boys' Club was unnecessary. Finally it was pointed out that a new Boys' Club in Belmont would have to be open to all youth in the general area and that this meant letting the Negroes and Puerto Ricans in. To resolve the conflict, a meeting was held for interested parties at which the representative of the head of Mt. Carmel Parish said that if the new facility was to be built, it should be named after Christopher Columbus, that a statue of Columbus, already on the property, should be incorporated in the overall design, and that bocci alleys should be provided for the old men. In October 1965 the new Boys' Club building and program in Belmont opened. It started with a predominantly Italian clientele. Within a year or two this arrangement was being vigorously questioned by various public officials. By spring 1968 it was filled with large numbers of Puerto Rican, Negro, *and* Italian youths.

The pastor of Mt. Carmel Parish at the time the Boys' Club was built, the man who built the present Mt. Carmel School in 1950, came to the United States from Sicily in 1920. He became pastor at Mt. Carmel in 1946, a monsignor in 1950, and an auxiliary bishop of the New York Archdiocese in 1954—a very successful church career in less than ten years after becoming pastor at Mt. Carmel. In 1968 he remained the only Catholic bishop of Italian background in the New York Archdiocese. In 1967 he was transferred from Mt. Carmel and promoted to the position of Archdiocesan Vicar of Putnam and Dutchess Counties, New York. The Mt. Carmel Church is and has been the central social institution in the Belmont community. For twenty years after World War II, it was led by a man who quickly became a bishop. Since he left the community, a number of local informants report he is sadly missed because of many of his virtues, including his political skill at protecting Belmont's interests —that is, its stakes in the urban game.[28]

Numerous other important local figures have always been found in Belmont. Many, like the bishop, have had and now have, careers in government, the professions, the unions, various industries, the rackets, education, and many other areas which have taken them far out of the Belmont community. But a very large number still return to work, to visit, to gather votes, and to do favors for what they define as their home community. Others continue to live and work in Belmont or to live there and work elsewhere. Such persons, together with their friends, relatives, and neighbors on the inside of that community, may be viewed as forming a powerful network of internal influence, leadership, and direction which, at the same time, also "connects" the people of Belmont to significant outside decision-making systems. To date, this network has enabled Belmont to protect its interests, but the process is becoming more difficult, with large measures of accommodation to outside interests now necessary.

East Tremont and Belmont: Their
Interrelationship and Differences

The troubles plaguing East Tremont result in part from the adamant stance taken by some of the Italians of Belmont in their efforts to resist what they define as the encroachments of nonwhite strangers pushing at the boundaries of their traditional enclave. Similarly, ethnocentrism and racial violence characteristic of some Belmont youths are aroused and exacerbated by the very presence of large numbers of Puerto Ricans and Negroes on the perimeter of the area and actually being introduced into neighborhood institutions, including the public schools, the playgrounds, and the Boys' Club. The relationship between the two communities may be described, therefore, as reciprocal. The Italians of Belmont did not create the present East Tremont ghetto, and the Puerto Ricans and Negroes of East Tremont certainly did not create Belmont. Both emerged in the course of the long-term growth and development of the Bronx and of New York City. Yet, in the mid-1960s, both communities are inextricably interrelated within the rapidly changing ecology of the Bronx, and the nature of the relationship is best defined as one of social conflict interlaced with constant, on-going accommodation. For example, much of the street violence which erupts and then subsides and then erupts again as more and more Puerto Ricans and Negroes enter the area is essentially a classic manifestation of the conflict-accommodation cycle. At the moment, a final resolution is hazardous to predict.

The differences between the two communities are profound. In terms of the framework and purpose of the present discussion, five central differences are most important.

First, the massive demographic transition characteristic of East Tremont has just begun to occur in Belmont. Although gradually declining in population in recent years, Belmont has just started the difficult process of changing, after more than fifty years of being a largely homogeneous ethnic enclave.

Second, in contrast to the serious institutional dislocations of East Tremont, Belmont's social institutions remain highly developed, coordinated, and functional. The description presented of Belmont stressed this community characteristic, with particular reference to youth needs and youth services, but it is also true of other facets of Belmont community life. What is not clear, at this point, is whether or not Belmont's institutions serve non-Italians as well as they serve Italians. The chances are that they do not.

Third, unlike East Tremont youth, the Italian young people of Belmont, whether on the blue-collar or white-collar career track, seem socially and psychologically relatively well integrated with their elders, both parents and other adults. This close generational "fit" is perhaps most clearly evident in the areas of education and employment, two institutional areas which in East Tremont are nothing less than chaotic in this and other respects.

Fourth, with the exception of some youthful violence against nonwhites and possibly some latent drift toward racketeering among the Italians of Belmont there appear to be no obvious adult cultural supports for delinquency and other forms of youthful deviation from middle-class norms. This sharply contrasts with what was found in East Tremont. It should be specifically noted, however, that in each community a strong adult community sentiment is present which condemns the delinquency patterns characteristic of the neighborhood.

Last, and perhaps most significant in terms of its political capacity to get what it wants and needs, East Tremont is grossly unskilled and structurally incapacitated. Belmont is not.

References

1. See Edwin H. Sutherland and Donald R. Cressey, *Principles of Criminology*, 7th ed. Philadelphia: Lippincott, 1966, pp. 15–16.
2. For a more complete discussion of this point, see *Report of the National Advisory Commission on Civil Disorders*. New York: Bantam, 1968.

3. Irving L. Horowitz and Martin Liebowitz, "Social Deviance and Political Marginality: Toward a Redefinition of the Relation Between Sociology and Politics," *Social Problems* 15:280–296 (Winter 1968).

4. Howard S. Becker, *Outsiders: Studies in the Sociology of Deviance*. New York: Free Press, 1963, especially Chaps. 1 and 2.

5. *Ibid.*, p. 9.

6. The invidious judgments of the middle class regarding the life style of lower-class communities, and the consequent attenuation of relationships between the people and the conventional institutions in the lower-class communities, are amply described in William F. Whyte, *Street Corner Society*. Chicago: University of Chicago Press, 1943; Herbert J. Gans, *The Urban Villagers*. New York: Free Press, 1962; and Becker, *op. cit*. The effect of such judgments on both individual and group is analyzed in considerable detail by Erving Goffman in *Stigma: Notes on the Management of Spoiled Identity*. Englewood Cliffs, N.J.: Prentice-Hall, 1963.

7. The issue involved in these terminological discussions is not new to the sociologist interested in crime and delinquency. For a classic treatment of the debate regarding legal and nonlegal definitions of crime and delinquency in sociological research, see Paul W. Tappan, "Who is the Criminal?" *American Sociological Review* 12:96–102 (February 1947).

8. Sophia M. Robison, *Can Delinquency Be Measured?* New York: Columbia University Press, 1936, p. 78.

9. *Ibid.*, pp. 96–99.

10. Alfred J. Kahn, *A Court for Children*. New York: Columbia University Press, 1953, pp. 108–109.

11. A further discussion of this point is found in *The Administration of Services to Children and Youth in New York City*. New York: Institute of Public Administration, 1963, pp. 25–56.

12. Kenneth B. Clark, *Dark Ghetto*. New York: Harper & Row, 1965, p. xv.

13. Maurice R. Stein, *The Eclipse of Community*. New York: Harper & Row, 1964, p. 125.

14. Jerome E. McElroy and John M. Martin, *The East Tremont Section of the Bronx: Delinquency as a Consequence of Struc-*

tural Change. New York: Fordham University, Juvenile Court Community Development Project, Working Paper, January 1968.

15. Edwin H. Sutherland, *The Professional Thief*. Chicago: University of Chicago Press, 1937, pp. iii–iv.

16. John M. Martin and Joseph P. Fitzpatrick, *Delinquent Behavior: A Redefinition of the Problem*. New York: Random House, 1965.

17. For a more general discussion of this same point, see *ibid.*, pp. 48–51.

18. Nathan Goldman, *The Differential Selection of Juvenile Offenders for Court Appearance*. New York: National Council on Crime and Delinquency, 1963.

19. James Q. Wilson, "The Police and the Delinquent in Two Cities," in Stanton Wheeler, ed., *Controlling Delinquents*. New York: Wiley, 1968, Chap. 2.

20. See, e.g., Marshall B. Clinard, *Slums and Community Development: Experiments in Self-Help*. New York: Free Press, 1966; Alfred J. Kahn, *Planning Community Services for Children in Trouble*. New York: Columbia University Press, 1963. For an early statement on the general problem, see Frederic M. Thrasher, *The Gang*, 2d rev. ed. Chicago: University of Chicago Press, 1936, especially Chaps. 22 and 23. A good recent design for a large-scale, local, self-help program with a political theme is found in *Youth in the Ghetto: A Study of the Consequences of Powerlessness and a Blueprint for Change*. New York: Harlem Youth Opportunities Unlimited, Inc., 1964.

21. A further discussion of this general point is found in Richard Hofstadter, *Social Darwinism in American Thought*, rev. ed. Boston: Beacon Press, 1955.

22. These statistics were published in *The New York Times*, January 29, 1968. The basic data released were reanalyzed in order to yield the information used to describe the 48th Police Precinct.

23. "Focal concern" is an anthropological concept which Walter B. Miller introduced into the delinquency field in his article, "Lower Class Culture as a Generating Milieu of Gang Delinquency," *Journal of Social Issues* 14:5–19 (1958). Miller de-

fined focal concerns as "areas or issues which command widespread and persistent attention and a high degree of emotional involvement." Miller is quite precise in articulating his reasons for choosing this concept instead of the concept of "value." ". . . (1) It is more readily derivable from direct field observation. (2) It is descriptively neutral—permitting independent consideration of positive and negative valences as varying under different conditions, whereas 'value' carried a built-in positive valence. (3) It makes possible more refined analysis of subcultural differences, since it reflects actual behavior, whereas 'value' tends to wash out intracultural differences since it is colored by notions of the 'official' ideal."

24. Data from *The New York Times,* December 23, 1966.

25. For an extended discussion of this same general concept, see Peter Marris and Martin Rein, *Dilemmas of Social Reform: Poverty and Community Action in the United States.* New York: Atherton Press, 1967, Chap. 2.

26. Henry D. McKay, "A Note on Trends in Rates of Delinquency in Certain Areas in Chicago," in *Task Force Report: Juvenile Delinquency and Youth Crime.* Washington, D.C.: The President's Commission on Law Enforcement and Administration of Justice, 1967, pp. 114–118.

27. See report by Richard Reeves, *The New York Times,* April 5, 1967.

28. A good recent case study of the urban game, as played by the mayor of New Haven, Connecticut, is provided by Allan R. Talbot, *The Mayor's Game.* New York: Harper & Row, 1967.

Chapter 5

SOME POLICY IMPLICATIONS OF THE NEW APPROACH

It should be clear that the structural approach to delinquency presented does not simply suggest minor changes in the existing practices of juvenile courts, juvenile correctional institutions, private youth-serving organizations of various sorts, and other agencies presently mandated to prevent and control delinquency. New formats for social investigations, reduction in the size of case loads, the advantages of group therapy, the use of halfway houses, or similar technical problems are not issues of major consequence. The structural approach is concerned with fundamental questions of policy: Will existing agencies dealing with delinquency continue to function to maintain, and to reinforce, the *status quo*—that is, will these agencies continue to remain committed to conservatism?[1] Or will these agencies, or many of them at least, come over to the side of domestic reform in the struggle for equality and justice for the nation's poor? If the latter goal is chosen, what strategies should be followed? What specific changes in agency organization and functioning should be addressed? What modifications in work role should professionals and others employed by such agencies begin to develop and apply?

The difficult and frequently exasperating task of changing the traditional tight case orientation and social control function of most existing delinquency agencies is only one facet of the job facing an agency that has made the decision to participate in alleviating social conditions adversely affecting disadvantaged youth. Gaining endorsement of an appropriate political constituency, including the poor themselves, to support an agency committed to social reform is a second facet of the task. The third is to get on with the work.

The following is offered as a broad statement of what policies need to be considered in applying the approach to delinquent behavior presented in this book. At least some of the policies may find application within both the public and private sectors of welfare as each relates itself to delinquency prevention and control. However, for the present, a few of the central policy positions set forth seem most applicable within the field of private welfare.* Later, when presently disadvantaged socio-ethnic groups have developed the political capacity to influence easily and directly public policy in the system of criminal justice, for example, the stress they may wish to put on developing strong systems of private welfare which they themselves own and operate may then be relaxed.

---

* "Private welfare," a term which still has considerable currency, may well be a misnomer. Many of today's "private welfare" agencies might better be described as "quasi-private" in that they depend for survival on substantial financial support from the public sector. On this point, see Charles F. Grosser, "Community Organization and the Grass Roots," *Social Work* 12:61–67 (October 1967).

Public Recognition of Social Conflict and Procedures for Mitigating Its Consequences

The first operating principle is the vigorous rejection of the premise that the major social norms governing the national society express the sentiments of the total collectivity. Conflicting norms within the larger society, such as those revealed by the sociogenic case history method, are readily identified. Clashing values on a broad scale are clearly visible. Given these conditions, it seems essential to recognize that, in many areas of society, subgroups within the system may accept prevailing norms only because powerful dominant groups have imposed these norms upon them by force or else because the subgroups have passively submitted to such norms.[2] Frequently, a deviant subgroup, such as nonconforming teen-agers, will subtly avoid confrontations, wherever feasible, and continue to adhere to its own standards. Sometimes the deviancy is massive and overt, as with recent wholesale looting during episodes of intense racial strife. With apparent strong support from many of their fellow ghetto-dwellers, the looters of the riots of 1964–1968, who were often young males from various socioeconomic segments of their home communities, seemed through their pilferage to be rejecting established patterns of white-black accommodation.[3] During the widespread riots of April 1968, the police, National Guard, and regular troops on riot control duty enacted a new master plan, which sought to contain civil disorders with a minimum of personal violence—a plan that temporarily set aside traditional law enforcement practices which have long defined property rights as superior to the human rights of property violators.[4] No doubt this devaluation of property by both looters and riot control personnel startled and bewildered many middle-class citizens who continue to hold tightly to their belief that private property is almost sacred.

Failure to recognize the existence, even the vitality, of normative conflicts among different segments of society makes it difficult for a program in the delinquency field to avoid the haz-

ards of an ethnocentric exercise of power. Despite the best inten-
tions, given programs may grind down upon their clientele.
Charity is no substitute for justice; compassion and understanding do not automatically bestow dignity; there is no substitute
for a fair share of the Gross National Product. The present,
almost completely unilateral process of decision-making by
agency personnel operating in juvenile courts and related public
and private agencies increases considerably the chance of unfairness.[5] Among the many contributing circumstances to such
unfairness, none is more significant than the fact that clients lack
effective and reliable representation of their interests. Their situations, problems, and point of view often do not receive adequate consideration. In such cases, when judges, psychiatrists,
social workers, and others with broad and frequently ill-defined
authority sit in judgment on adolescents and their families sus-
pected of social deviation and when the adjudged are poor
Negroes, Puerto Ricans, or members of other politically disadvantaged groups, the risk of *mis*judgment and even prejudicial
condemnation is acute. Descriptions of the chaos in the Criminal
Court of the City of New York give a frightening picture of the
"nonadministration" of justice,[6] which is even more appalling
when it is realized that the great majority of those abused by the
system are Negroes and Puerto Ricans. And the same disorder
along similar dominant-minority group axes repeats itself in
many different jurisdictions. Similar risks are present, of course,
even when socially deviant groups drawn from the white middle
class, such as present-day hippies and college draft resisters, are
judged by officials. When those doing the judging are committed,
consciously or not, to preserving the interests and sentiments of
the dominant strata and seemingly are unaware that these norms
and values are not shared by other groups within the society,
then actual injustice may be done. Moreover, since the effects of
official treatment may often be hazardous for the individual and
of doubtful rehabilitative benefit, the influence of the system of
criminal justice cannot be presumed to be benevolent. This was
clearly recognized, for example, in the recent Gault decision by
the United States Supreme Court, which critically reviewed the

malevolent consequences of prevailing juvenile court practice.[7]

The manner in which unfairness may find expression in the delinquency field is highlighted in Chapter 2 on situational analysis. There, serious cross-cultural contradictions found in the juvenile court and juvenile corrections are described as barriers between the judged and those who judge them and interpret their behavior.

The way in which welfare services and other community resources may be differentially distributed among the various ethnic groups in a great city is discussed in Chapter 4. That the poorest should end up with the fewest resources is not surprising; it is simply another sign of their deprivation. The same chapter compares two contemporary and adjacent Bronx neighborhoods and contrasts their capacities to organize to meet the needs of their children and youth. The Italian community of Belmont is besieged by the upsetting changes of the mid-twentieth-century Bronx. Consequently, it is now rapidly changing. This should not blur the fact, however, that, as a community committed to its own self-interest, Belmont has for a long period been able to get and hold what it wants. Neighborhoods such as the East Tremont ghetto, it seems, need to develop "institutionalized power" * in order to achieve what Belmont has accomplished, without developing Belmont's vigorous ethnocentrism. If both sides of this delicate equation cannot be mastered at the same time, then for the sake of their own self-interests, communities such as East Tremont may simply need to be encouraged to play the American game of power politics and let the more advantaged communities fend for themselves. Past history and present events show that the more advantaged usually make out well no matter what happens.

When agencies of criminal justice attempt to understand and otherwise relate to offenders drawn from the seriously disadvantaged strata of society, they face many complex problems. A technical examination of what might be called the discontinui-

---

* "Institutionalized power" may be defined as collective, as opposed to personal or individual, power; it is also sustained, organized, recognized, and utilized power, which is wielded by an interest group.

ties in the theory and practice of correctional casework reveals one aspect of these difficulties. The dependence of the correctional field, both adult and juvenile, upon social casework methods for a systematic probing of individual cases makes any flaw in these methods extremely significant. Such a flaw affects the entire process of social investigation and recommendation, sentencing or disposition, and rehabilitation, confinement, and release. The usual casework methods appear to be almost completely concerned with the adjustment of the individual to prevailing social standards, rigorously defined in middle-class terms. Yet they operate under the guise of an idealized model of case analysis, which is essentially a scaled-down application of psychodynamic psychiatry. Psychodynamic psychiatry stresses *intrapersonal* psychic adjustment as a basis for change in individual functioning. To a surprising degree, casework methods in correction end up doing something quite different: they measure and stress overt conformity to middle-class standards, values, and life styles. These conclusions are amply supported by a content analysis of significant instructional manuals in the field, such as *The Presentence Investigation Report*[8] distributed by the Administrative Office of the United States Courts in 1965; the influential 1960 book by Paul Keve, *The Probation Officer Investigates*;[9] and the *Casebook in Correctional Casework*[10] published by the Council on Social Work Education in 1958.

It may be that the nation in its conventional wisdom intends to use and enforce middle-class norms, values, and life styles when it requires that authorities make judgments about who is to get what kind of treatment or sentence, as the case may be, in the criminal justice system. It may consider these to be the norms, values, and life styles which represent the consensus of the citizens and which must be enforced as the basis of the national life. Clearly, when these standards are enforced, the socially, culturally, and politically disadvantaged will suffer, since they will be coerced into conformity. No orderly society can avoid this human phenomenon. The Mormons were compelled to give up the practice of polygamy because they did not have the political strength to support their set of values; critics of the

Vietnam war today are being compelled to accept the military draft as a fact of life, since the established government and its constituency support this position. If this is the principle which guides the official handling of delinquents, it should be openly stated and enforced, not disguised as an aspect of good mental hygiene. It really has nothing to do with mental hygiene, good or bad. It is a problem of a conflict of values and the issue is the extent to which the community at large is willing to admit the legitimacy of norms and values peculiar to one subgroup or subculture in its midst. When these conflicts of value are made explicit, political processes exist by which they can be accommodated or resolved, sometimes, as noted, by legal coercion. Real damage, however, is done not only to delinquent youth, but also to society at large, when one segment of the population, one ethnic group or social class, identifies its *own* definition of values as the national consensus and proceeds to enforce it. This can easily become a practice of politically enforced ethnocentrism or the protection of class interests. There is abundant evidence that, in the correction of delinquents, this is often the case.

A sound public policy designed to remove unfair practices from the system of criminal justice cannot tolerate this or other forms of dominant-group ethnocentrism, where they have become institutionalized in correctional practice. This means that the very models of social investigation and treatment most agencies use in judging delinquents and in doing something to or for them are incompatible with a sound system of legal justice. Through the use of drastic new models and within a wide range of normative limits specifying what contemporary American society will not tolerate in adolescent behavior, new dimensions of pluralistic tolerance might be built into day-to-day decision-making in the delinquency field. But more than cultural pluralism is needed. The structural nature of the delinquency problem, especially among the disadvantaged, also needs to be considered, not only in terms of relevant psychic and familial variables, but also in terms of their relationship to a wide range of personal, social, and cultural variables at the level of the reference group and neighborhood and in terms of the greater community itself. It would be best to examine each youth in these terms, in order to understand him properly in the context of his own community. The assessment methodology specified in this book offers one means by which this may now be done.

However, studying cases in isolation is not sufficient. An environmentally oriented agency policy requires recognition of the fact that most official delinquents tend to come from urban slums and that the cases originating in any given slum, or section thereof, need to be studied *collectively*. This would permit diagnostically relevant patterns to emerge and would reveal links between individual cases. It would also show the relationship between individual case data and prevailing environmental conditions. And most significant, the malfunctioning of the local environment itself could then become an object of investigation, as well as the malignant relationship of this environment to the wider community. If this line of analysis were initiated, new programs aimed at creating environmental change, as a central objective of delinquency agency function, might then logically follow. Conservative and narrow self-interests may insist that institutional reforms must not occur or, as it is more often put, that all changes be slow, gradual, and nondisruptive. Translated pragmatically, this means no real change at all. This view may prevail for a year or for a decade or two, but not forever. The ebb and flow of reform in America testifies that nothing, and nobody, is capable of stopping indefinitely the acquisition of power by shut-out sectors of the population. And with power achieved, suitable institutional rearrangements usually follow.

Modern American ghettos, where official delinquency is concentrated, need almost everything in the way of environmental change and social reform. Almost anything that can be accomplished in this regard is an improvement over what is now there. But from the vantage point of the structural analysis of delinquent behavior, several new forms of programming appear to be essential in order to reduce sharply delinquency in urban slums. Each would certainly constitute a vital aspect of any community development-type program put into effect by a delinquency agency.

The first is obvious: a massive national outpouring for urban slum people of welfare, educational, housing, and work programs. The magnitude of this task is well described in the *Report of the National Advisory Commission on Civil Disorders*.[11] No less than this scale of "ultimate prevention" [12] seems capable of effectively addressing the fundamental institutional dislocations lying at the root of ghetto deprivation. The Negro violence which struck well over a hundred cities during April 1968 should remove the last vestige of doubt that only sustained national action can end the enduring crisis of the ghetto.

On the level of the local ghetto, highly specific programs clearly need to be established for a variety of purposes, including the delivery and fair distribution to all disadvantaged minorities of the national wealth which seems destined to be reallocated to slum communities. From region to region, from city to city, from neighborhood to neighborhood, the needs are so widespread that no one group among the poor, no one neighborhood among a large city's many slums, should be given preferential treatment. The discussion here will be about new types of welfare programs and their delivery systems which seem particularly suited to two tasks: (1) meeting the goal of a fair distribution of resources on an intracity basis, as these might be allocated for the purpose of doing something significant about urban delinquency; and (2) developing and administering in the most efficient manner neighborhood welfare programs specifically designed to prevent and control delinquency among slum children and youth. The complex and difficult problem of maintaining a fair distribution of resources on a regional or intercity basis would have to be resolved by other means which will not be considered here.

The identification of high-priority delinquency areas within a particular city is an ecological problem which may be resolved by methods similar to the ones presented in Chapter 3 on area analysis. Using police or court records and other population data, the most seriously disadvantaged neighborhoods with the highest concentrations of official delinquents can be plotted and described by any agency, public or private, interested in doing the job.

Once high-priority neighborhoods have been identified, new types of locally based welfare programs might be mounted in such areas. These locally based programs would have three general purposes. First, they would be designed to meet a number of the self-defined reality needs of ghetto youth and at the same time act to prevent the spread of alienation and the outbreak of serious delinquency among such youth.

Second, these programs, if administratively situated outside the system of criminal justice in the so-called private sector of welfare, could be used to divert local youth out of the official system when they got "in trouble." Thus modern ghetto-dwellers could follow the lead presented by the Jews, Irish Catholics, and other earlier immigrant groups who developed their own large-scale private welfare systems which served to divert their children and youth from the courts, public training schools, and reformatories of earlier days. Such local programs might not only help local youth in some worthy welfare sense, but they might also, quite literally, be used, wherever feasible, to keep local youths out of official trouble by taking them out of the hands of overworked police youth bureaus and precincts, off the overcrowded dockets of juvenile courts, and otherwise out of the official processes of justice. Just such a mechanism for local communities was recommended by the President's Commission on Law Enforcement and Administration of Justice in the form of local Youth Services Bureaus.[13] Such bureaus, the commission urged, should be situated in comprehensive neighborhood community centers and should receive juveniles, both delinquent and nondelinquent, referred by the police, the juvenile court, parents, schools, and other sources. Linked with juvenile court policies designed to narrow the court's jurisdiction to more serious offenders and to policies designed to dispose of as many cases as possible without official adjudication, such bureaus could deal much more informally with many local adolescents defined as deviant.

One of the significant similarities between the concept of

Youth Services Bureaus offered by the President's commission and the concept being developed here is that both recommend that the parent structures operating such services in local communities might best be situated administratively outside of the network of public agencies. Sponsored and operated to a maximum extent by local community residents, such services would be offered in the private welfare sector, but not by those groups and organizations which now run things in private welfare. Ideally, the new services would be run by those sectors of the nation's population whose members most often inhabit urban slums and whose children and youth most often are arrested, sent to court, and committed to correctional institutions. In plain language, this means that in Washington, D.C., Chicago, New York City, Boston, and scores of other cities, north and south, the Blacks, Puerto Ricans, and other presently disadvantaged groups in the ghettos of these communities would develop the capacities to own, operate, and staff the new local services.

This leads to the third, and perhaps the most significant, purpose which could be served by local, privately controlled welfare services to ghetto youth. Such service delivery systems could themselves become increasingly important bases of institutionalized power for presently disadvantaged groups, which could use these service structures and the taxes which would support them to help create their own welfare enterprises. Following an argument advanced by Frances Piven and Richard Cloward, private agencies of this order would be as much political as social welfare institutions, inasmuch as they would serve as organizational vehicles for the expression of the group's viewpoints on social welfare policy and also as the means for other forms of political association and influence.[14] Once developed, the strength of these new welfare organizations, working in combination with similar local and community-wide enterprises in education, health, religion, and other fields, could be used by the disadvantaged to improve their own general bargaining position vis-à-vis other, more established, interest groups. It is the enhancement of this bargaining position and the consequent enrichment and empathic modification of institutions and practices that offers the key to social change in the ghetto. The accomplishment of this kind of change is the goal of those who would take a structural approach to delinquency and related social problems.

This general course of action has been followed in the past, and remains the case today, in New York, for example, with the Catholics, Jews, and also, of course, with the white Protestants. The political advantages to be gained by today's disadvantaged groups through the development of their own, privately controlled, tax-supported welfare delivery systems cannot be matched by launching new programs and continuing old programs for the disadvantaged through long-established agencies, either public or private, particularly where the recipients of service exercise little or no voice in policy. Put bluntly, the issue is one of control and influence: Who is going to run what for whom? And consequently, who is going to profit politically, psychologically, economically, and in many other ways from the enterprise?

Indigenous minority leaders say that what they want is *money* and *dignity*. Some say they want *power*. The right kinds of welfare, education, housing, and work are four good vehicles for obtaining all three. The right kind of locally controlled welfare agency seems to be one very good device which a neighborhood might use to compete successfully for these types of broadly scaled programs, many of which will have to be paid for by state and federal monies. Such highly diverse and specialized programs, once obtained, need not necessarily be run by the local welfare agencies which were instrumental in securing them. Welfare is only one institutional set in any community and certainly not the largest. Other locally controlled institutions in education and in housing, for example, might operate their own nonwelfare neighborhood programs. This division of labor would keep each separate institutional set focused upon its own area of expertise, much as is the case in the broader community. Such an arrangement of minority-group power, with the proper political coordination at both the neighborhood and wider community levels, might actually provide greater stability and strength for a ghetto than one giant, omnipotent, neighborhood agency. In any case, once a locally run ghetto agency is brought into being in the private sector of welfare, the people who own it can decide which particular political strategy they may wish to follow at any given time.

Until locally owned welfare agencies can be run on an independent basis in slum communities, it will probably be necessary for coalitions of more powerful groups and institutions to work closely with disadvantaged people in various neighborhoods to design, establish, operate, and fund such enterprises. Funding offers an apt illustration of the difficulties which disadvantaged groups are likely to experience in creating such organizations on their own. Except for antipoverty money, which is very unstable and not a large part of any city or state operating budget, most of the stable funding patterns in education, welfare, and medical care—to cite three crucial areas—are not now within the grasp of the disadvantaged. As is the case in manufacturing, banking, defense, higher education, and other great American industries, the disadvantaged are also seriously disadvantaged when they try to own and operate any major sector of private welfare. If properly qualified, they may be either the recipients or the social workers of private welfare, but they are not yet able to own the structures dispensing the services. Given this state of affairs, coalitions which join together the disadvantaged and the advantaged are probably not only desirable but necessary for establishing the type of local welfare agency described above.[15] Some might believe that such coalitions are in fact highly desirable in their own right on a permanent basis, since they may serve to reduce the polarization of racial conflict now openly characteristic of many American cities. That may or may not be true. It does seem, however, that such coalitions are pragmatically essential for enabling the disadvantaged to get at the resources of money, professional expertise, and institutionalized power necessary for bringing effective local programs on a massive scale into urban ghettos. Participation at all levels—from policy-making to typing—in such coalitions by representatives of the disadvantaged could, in turn, serve to direct the content of the new programs and to prevent them from becoming just another phase of the domestic colonialism now so characteristic of ghetto life. Starting as full partners, these participants could progressively take over larger measures of control and responsibility. The design would call for effective transfer of program ownership, from the advantaged to the disadvantaged, with all possible speed.

New Roles for Delinquency Prevention and Control Workers

A second program priority for coping with urban delinquency and the many problems associated with it involves the articulation of new work roles for both professionals and nonprofessionals working in such programs. The most difficult technical innovation required would be the development and allocation of agency workers who could systematically assess delinquency in structural terms, using a methodology similar to the approach presented in the preceding chapters. Actually, the other new work roles required to get the job done are not very new at all, except that they are not usually found in the repertoire of professional roles played by most social workers, psychiatrists, psychologists, and vocational counselors who, among others, would be called upon to man the new programs. *Mediators, advocates, activists*, and *community organizers*—to name some of the specific work roles involved—are scarcely new job titles in American society, past or present.[16] This is perhaps more clearly evident when these roles are briefly defined. Each definition will be tailored to fit the role as it might be applied within the framework of delinquency prevention and control in the slum. Each might be applied at the level of an individual youth defined as "troublesome" or at the level of a pressing social issue affecting youth in the ghetto, depending upon time, place, and need. Of the four roles described, and the list is not meant to be exhaustive, only that of community organizer seems to be essentially group-oriented, as opposed to the others which might operate at both the group and individual levels. It also seems fairly clear that any given worker may be called upon to play one or more of these roles, in addition to the conventional ones he already possesses, as he commits himself to the cause of slum youth.

—*Mediators:* bridgemen who settle disputes between disadvantaged youth and others, especially outside authorities, usually with the consent of both parties.

—*Advocates:* partisans who vigorously argue for disadvantaged youth, particularly against the representatives of the advantaged.

—*Activists:* doers who get things started case by case and issue by issue until needs are articulated and action initiated.

—*Community organizers:* leaders who convene and facilitate political action at both the grassroots and community-wide levels to resolve institutional dislocations facing slum youth.

Labor unions, business organizations, universities, churches, the press, and government, among other significant social institutions, have always found room for such talents. Key traits characterizing such role occupants have been their militancy and their intransigency, once committed to a course of action which each defined as in his own self-interest or those of his particular constituency.

Even social work, before it became so dependent upon clinical psychiatry, had its own social reformers who were committed to institutional change in the name of the poor through mediation, advocacy, activism, community organization, or otherwise correcting misalignments in existing structural arrangements. The problem is that, with few exceptions, most present-day agencies in the delinquency field remain so tightly wedded to the so-called one-to-one approach, working for individual rehabilitation through personal attitudinal change, that they have forgotten all about the problems of the social structure which so fascinated the pioneer muckrakers. Today these same problems concern a growing number of social workers, mainly the young just entering the profession, but their commitment to social reform remains largely personal and *aprofessional*. This is especially true among caseworkers, who constitute the bulk of the profession. Their training and their agencies have failed to provide them with perspectives and concrete social change program models, both of which remain grossly underdeveloped. Instead, the conventional tendency in social welfare has been to evaluate delinquency and other forms of deviant behavior in therapeutic, rather than political, terms.[17] And work roles in agency practice were fashioned accordingly.

Today, however, a new movement is joining together dissident social workers[18] with an increasing number of social scientists, a few lawyers, and other professionals. Organized, purposeful, political action for social change has all but captivated the thinking of this "New Left" to which many minority people and alienated youth also belong. Delinquency agencies and related facets of the criminal justice system have been slow in keeping up with the revolutionary movement building up in and outside of the welfare field during the last ten years. Such organizations, firmly routinized in their own traditions of individual responsibility, punishment, protection of society, and individual rehabilitation, cannot be expected to adapt themselves easily to the task of social reform. Many find it threatening even to contemplate leaving the security of the courthouse or reformatory to establish meaningful on-the-spot communications with ghetto people. But then, too, particular agencies, especially those in the delinquency field *per se,* which traditionally have been more flexible than those dealing with adult crime, should not be counted out too soon. For example, some professional work roles in a few delinquency agencies are slowly shifting as community organizers, sometimes surreptitiously, are being hired as regular staff. Lawyers for the poor are being engaged. Even sociologists, long viewed by many social workers as a menace to their own professional interests, are being offered jobs, usually as researchers in established criminal justice agencies. The day may come when even economists and political scientists will be asked to participate. Unfortunately, the number of lawyers and social scientists available for such positions is and will remain very small, and the number actually hired, due to a variety of organizational strictures, even smaller. Moreover, most agencies will, for a long time, be incapable of quickly absorbing very many of this new breed of welfare worker.

What probably will occur and what probably is, in fact, already occurring, is that those agencies which are not opting out of the new movement toward social reform are already gradually shifting the work roles of their existing staffs in the new direction. Sometimes by design, sometimes not, caseworkers are beginning to act like advocates, group workers are being called upon to function as community organizers and activists, and a few psychiatrists are speaking out about the inefficiency of their conventional techniques in working with the poor and the dissident. Some shifts in the psychiatrist's work role, which has long been central in the delinquency field, are already occurring.

Two basic changes in psychiatric practice seem particularly appropriate for working with disadvantaged youth "in trouble." First, building on a broader approach, such as the one outlined in this book, a new interpersonal theory of personality is essential, one which would enable the practitioner to evaluate an adolescent's delinquency within the value system and norms of that adolescent's particular community. Furthermore, the new theory would need to consider the adolescent's neighborhood milieu and his place in it in terms of the various institutional dislocations characteristic of the area.

Psychiatrists now generally do not have the specialized training to view a slum community in depth, taking full recognition of the social and cultural variables which shape the personality and influence the behavior of slum residents. When these social and cultural variables are fully understood, the change in psychiatric approach (within the framework of sociogenic theory) may be most profound. For example, when the psychiatric method outlined in Chapter 1 was applied to the cases studied and described in this book, it was usually found that fewer and

less severe psychiatric disorders were present than had been diagnosed by the court psychiatrists who studied the same adolescents.

A second major change in psychiatric practice is also directly related to a practitioner's ability to understand the full
impact of environment, broadly defined, upon an adolescent's
personality and behavior. The traditional psychiatrist has long
associated delinquency with mental illness. Even the more culturally oriented psychiatrist has tended to view delinquency *a
priori* as symptomatic of personality disturbance. This has been
especially true when personality disturbances have been noted
among delinquent populations in various agency settings. This
assumption led quite naturally to a treatment program which
essentially consisted of one-to-one therapy, or sometimes group
therapy, for the delinquent. The results of this program have not
been gratifying. Moreover, and most important, this approach
did nothing about preventing the development of delinquent behavior in the young. With the help of the methods described in
this book, it now becomes possible for the psychiatrist, when
psychiatric illness is present in a delinquent youth, to delineate
whether the delinquency is a manifestation of the personality
disturbance or is in fact unrelated to it. It also becomes easier
for the therapist to evaluate the degree to which personality
problems (mental illness) in the young may be caused or influenced by minority status, membership in deprived subcultures,
and other socially stressful conditions. This should suggest to
the psychiatrist that conventional psychiatric treatment, as such,
for the kind of youngster caught up in such conditions is inappropriate. A variety of social and cultural variables in his life are
dynamically active in producing problems which psychoanalyti-
cally oriented psychotherapy is simply not designed to solve.

Robert Gould's work with blue-collar laborers in an auto
union illustrates some of the modifications a psychiatrist may
employ in treating patients from a social class and culture different from his own.[19] However, when delinquency exists as a way
of life and is not reflective of mental illness, treatment on a one-

to-one or group basis is again inappropriate. Other approaches to the handling of delinquency are needed.

The psychiatrist also needs to realize that systems set up by the power structure, which discriminate against culturally disadvantaged and deprived youngsters, must themselves be changed in attitude and function. These include many schools, courts, and police, and, indeed, other arms of the established community which reach into the lives of these youngsters. The psychiatrist is then charged with the responsibility of applying his psychiatric knowledge of what influences personality development to an examination of prevailing systems and their relationship to personality. In doing this, he will need to tackle the difficult job of changing these systems into constructive forces rather than allowing them to remain irrelevant, misunderstanding, hostile, or punitive forces, which themselves often contribute to delinquency.

For example, in a school where an adolescent speaks English poorly and where teachers may harbor attitudes ranging from indifference to outright hostility, disdain, or even fear, the milieu is a noxious one. To make it worse, the school may also be overcrowded, operating on triple sessions, and filled with conflicting racial factions among the students. Escaping from such conditions through truancy is a natural response for an adolescent. Such a school is only one of the many systems which may thus "contribute" to what society calls "delinquency."

The juvenile justice system too may be viewed as an arm of the established classes—both in the values on which it is based and in the kinds of people who, as its judges, social workers, psychiatrists, and custodial personnel, are vested with the power to enforce these values. The courts, probation, correctional institutions, and parole all rank high on the list of systems which often humiliate, misunderstand, and oppress the disadvantaged young offenders with whom they deal. Frequently their efforts to rehabilitate, even when of high professional quality, are irrelevant to the pressing reality needs of the juveniles involved. Such treatment may cause further alienation in such youngsters, leading them again to act out against the established community in ways that again will be defined as "delinquency."

The connection between delinquency and mental illness is not a simple one; the two may be parallel, complementary, or overlapping. Although delinquent behavior may well be a manifestation or symptom of a personality warp, in certain subcultural settings such behavior develops as a natural style of life, without indicating psychological impairment *per se*. This is not to say, however, that this kind of behavior is reflective of good mental health simply because it is culturally "normal." For some members of disadvantaged minority groups, constant exposure to subjugation, discrimination, or prejudice may seriously undermine their self-esteem, thus directly attacking a crucial and basic variable in good mental health. The environmental conditions which are contributing to behavior termed "delinquent" may also set the stage for emotional difficulties. Furthermore, the ways in which various official systems react to a youngster's delinquency may themselves contribute further to his poor mental health and to his continued delinquency. Punishment, ostracism, and lack of sympathetic understanding serve to deepen feelings of inadequacy, alienation, or low self-esteem. Even efforts to help, if made in a form of treatment that is ineffective or irrelevant, produce increased feelings of confusion, unworthiness, and frustration and may end by hindering the youngster's attempt to become a healthy, well-functioning person in his society. But the problem does not stop here. At the same time, those responsible for the subjugation, discrimination, and prejudice are also, ironically, very likely doing violence to their own mental health. The hurts suffered by the oppressed are shared by their oppressors, for both are participants in the same system—one which fosters individual delinquency, collective violence, and other manifestations of the present urban crisis. On some level, the "advantaged" majority feels guilt, shame, and a sense of failure for its role, whether active or passive, in what in many ways is emerging as a brutal national society.

The implications for psychiatry are clear. A better understanding of the relationship of a specific instance of delinquent behavior and personality disorder is possible through the broader approach being presented.

To the extent that environmental conditions contribute to delinquent behavior, psychiatry might well address itself not to the individual who, in the cultural sense, is "doing what comes naturally," but to the systems which generate this behavior both in his own subculture and in the larger, often oppressing, dominant society. This means that the psychiatrist would have to familiarize himself with such institutions as those involved in housing, employment, education, and the judicial and correctional processes. He would also need to study their influence on personality development and mental health. Working with others, he could then take the necessary steps to try to change unhealthy processes in these various structures. Social action of this kind is mandatory if real shifts in the attitude and functions of these institutions are to occur.*

The psychiatrist, in participating in social action, will be drawn into political arenas which he has largely shunned in his traditional role of therapist. However, many political, economic, and other social factors are interwoven with the interpersonal familial factors in the fabric of personality structure. If the psychiatrist is really to treat the whole person, as he claims to do, then he will need to understand and influence those conditions which have until now remained outside his sphere of influence and, perhaps, interest. All of them play important roles in the

---

* It is perhaps significant to note in this regard that a recent lead article in the journal of the National Association of Social Workers called for the disengagement of much social work manpower from its present deployment in welfare organizations to nonwelfare organizations such as education, housing, and health. Once so redeployed, social workers would not engage in the caretaking and rehabilitation of people who are deprived, ill, and unskilled, but instead would work directly to alter the dysfunctional aspects of the systems within which they were employed. To succeed in this new task, social workers would need to be knowledgeable about the specific area in which they worked, e.g., housing, health, education, in addition to their usual knowledge about individual and family functioning. John B. Turner, "In Response to Change: Social Work at the Crossroad," *Social Work* 13:7–15 (July 1968).

development of good and bad mental health. This is only another aspect of what psychiatry can and should be doing in the community.

The movement in the management of delinquency would seem to require changing directions from treatment of the already formed delinquent—a method which reaches few youngsters, over long periods, with indifferent results—to a more preventive method of psychiatry, which would intervene at early levels and influence the various conditions in the minority and dominant communities which are related to delinquent activity.

A number of other important work role shifts are necessary for gaining an effective understanding of delinquency among slum youth. For example, the whole question of "field-centered," rather than "office-centered," interviewing by social workers and psychiatrists applying the recommended new approach is fundamental for effective data-gathering. These highly trained professionals must learn to apply their skills in the streets, apartments, and rooming houses and in the poolrooms and other hangouts of the adolescents they are seeking to understand. According to the principles of the approach being discussed, there simply is no substitute for first-hand observation of slum life as experienced by disadvantaged youth.

Obviously, deep personal and organizational strains will emerge when radical changes of the types described begin to occur in agency work roles. The development of these strains gives rise to the third program priority to be discussed.

Integration of the New Work Roles with Delinquency Agency Structure

The personal commitment of some individual workers to new work roles aimed at social reform is no substitute for a cool, calculated, total agency commitment to the same goal. Yet this shift in agency policy and in associated and necessary work role modifications for agency personnel will not occur easily nor without high cost, both organizational and financial. Employees will quit or be fired; new friends will be won and new enemies made; more, not less, money will be spent.

However, once an agency decides that it wants to, that in fact it must, run these risks, then new policy orientations must be acquired, new skills and methods mastered, and, above all, new standards for worker supervision and general agency strategy articulated and enforced. No social caseworker, for example, in a psychiatric clinic accepting disadvantaged Negro and Puerto Rican youngsters, can act effectively as an advocate for a needy case against outside institutional interests unless the clinic in which she is working is itself organized to perform this function. Clinic policy makers must understand and support such activity. A whole new professional ethos, methodology, and interlock of various agency work roles must be created to encourage a caseworker to take such action, as a fundamental part of her job in the field of mental health, as she relates to her disadvantaged clients. For example, if the caseworker's supervisor does not consider such activity to be proper professional behavior in the setting of a psychiatric clinic, then the caseworker-advocate is in for a hard time. If the psychiatrists for whom the caseworker works do not see the relevance of advocacy to the mental health needs of disadvantaged minority youngsters who are their patients, then the caseworker-advocate role becomes virtually impossible. Even with the best of agency organizational supports, if the same caseworker has not been professionally trained to look systematically for the need for advocacy in the various cases of disadvantaged youngsters with whom she works and if she has not been taught what effective action to take with regard to outside forces which may be grinding down upon her client and his family, then the caseworker can only act as an *amateur* advocate, not as a professional one. And the same is true for·caseworkers, psychiatrists, psychologists, educators, and related professionals working in other agencies such as training schools, juvenile courts, and similar delinquency settings. They are really no better off than the psychiatric caseworker just described, unless new shifts in their work roles are strongly and meaningfully supported by the organizational and professional structures within which they work. In sum, the third program priority requires that emergent new work roles be supported by well-developed agency strategies and functions. Perhaps the best single word to describe the militant agency stance required toward social justice and client rights is that the agency must be, as the "Ricans" say, *guapo*—that is, tough, in the sense that labor unions are tough.[20] Moreover, the professions involved need to be not only ideologically committed to the same goals when they speak and act with respect to the disadvantaged, but they also need to provide their practitioners with relevant job training and skills.

Proper modification of professional training and skills requires far more than agencies can deliver, even when they are owned and operated by representatives of the disadvantaged. Education in schools of social work, in law, in medical schools and psychiatric residencies, in sociology and political science, to name some of the more central disciplines involved, will also have to be changed if the challenge of the new movement is to be well met. New courses will be required in such areas as these: the structural analysis of delinquency; the whole question of deviancy as it becomes socially defined; the law of the poor; the politics of welfare; and finally, a new interpersonal theory of psychiatry encompassing psychology, sociology, and cultural anthropology. That a few such courses are beginning to appear in the catalogues of some schools of social work and law, for example, is evidence that universities are beginning to respond to these needs. New teams of professors will probably have to be formed to bring into the same classroom the multidisciplinary expertise necessary to develop and teach effectively almost any of these new courses. Finally, proper training in research, in professional practice, and in subject matter per se will require that on-going field experiences in newly oriented practice agencies will have to be developed to provide graduate students with firsthand experience with their newly emerging, professional work roles. The educational needs are great and, in many respects, can never be fully met. But the alternative—no change at all—is, to many, simply unacceptable.

Even more is necessary. The degree of sophistication required to plan and execute the recommended types of new community programs demands much closer cooperation between universities and operating agencies than is needed for the training of future professionals. Universities themselves are important sources of power and prestige within their communities. Despite the many difficulties surrounding a university's involvement in "town" affairs, no great urban university can remain aloof from the domestic scene today. Few, in fact, have remained silent when the march of urban blight has reached their own thresholds. Involvement versus noninvolvement is not the issue. The manner of involvement and the side of the commitment are really what are at stake.*

In a more technical sense, there is still another link between urban universities and community programs of the kinds being described. It is the urban universities which, in their various schools, departments, and research institutes, house the full range of multidisciplinary experience so badly needed for planning, developing, and advancing new kinds of national policy to meet the challenge of the urban ghetto. It is in the nearby university that local agency administrators are most likely to find the range of skills needed to help with the design, execution, and the rigorous on-going evaluation of their radically new kinds of urban welfare programs. It is through stable day-to-day working relationships between university professors and agency staff that model delinquency programs of the type suggested have the best chance of realization and fulfillment. The disadvantaged cannot do it alone. The agencies cannot do it alone either. Nor, certainly, can the universities. However, different mixes of the three would seem to provide a good working nucleus around which could be formed wider coalitions capable of making significant

---

* Obviously, the question of the relationship between universities—understood in terms of their trustees, administrators, faculties, students, and alumni—and the problems of the inner city is complex, little explored, and brimming with many unsolved, even unspecified, issues. Just as obviously, the subject of university-inner city relations, although introduced, cannot be considered more than tangentially in the present discussion.

advances with the type of program strategy specified. Crucial to the success of these efforts would be the commitment of responsive divisions of government, industry, and other centers of national power.

This book is offered as a statement of what is involved in converting agencies operating in the delinquency field into forces which can take a structural approach to delinquency. The orientation, assessment methodology, and the policy recommendations presented give one view of what might be done to understand better and meet the challenge of delinquent behavior. The orientation and methodology presented, or some adaptation of them, in a technical sense are now capable of being implemented at the level of concrete action. Whether they will in fact find expression through changes in public policy remains, of course, a political, not a scientific, question.

References

1. For this definition of conservatism, see Lewis A. Coser, *Continuities in the Study of Social Conflict*. New York: Free Press, 1967, pp. 156–157.
2. *Ibid.*, p. 164.
3. E. L. Quarantelli and Russell R. Dynes, "Looting in Civil Disorders: An Index of Social Change," *American Behavioral Scientist* 2:7–10 (March–April 1968). Other articles in the same issue are also devoted to the topic, "Urban Violence and Disorder." See also the *Report of the National Advisory Commission on Civil Disorders*. New York: Bantam, 1968, pp. 127–135.
4. See report by Ben A. Franklin, *The New York Times*, April 14, 1968.
5. The legal injustice inherent in the nation's present system of juvenile justice has for more than two decades been noted by a select group of scholars. A good recent discussion of this issue is

found in David Matza, *Delinquency and Drift*. New York: Wiley, 1964, Chap. 4.

6. See report by Edward C. Burks, *The New York Times*, February 12, 1968.

7. *Gault v. U.S.* 18 L. ed. 2nd. 527,87 SCT (May 15, 1967).

8. *The Presentence Investigation Report*. Washington, D.C.: Division of Probation, Administrative Office of the United States Courts, 1965.

9. Paul W. Keve, *The Probation Officer Investigates: A Guide to the Presentence Report*. Minneapolis: University of Minnesota Press, 1960.

10. *Casebook in Correctional Casework*. New York: Committee on Corrections, Council on Social Work Education, 1958.

11. *Report of the National Advisory Commission on Civil Disorders*, *op. cit.*, Chap. 17.

12. For a further discussion of this concept, see John M. Martin and Joseph P. Fitzpatrick, *Delinquent Behavior: A Redefinition of the Problem*. New York: Random House, 1965, p. 178.

13. *The Challenge of Crime in a Free Society*. Washington, D.C.: President's Commission on Law Enforcement and Administration of Justice, February 1967, Chap. 3.

14. Frances Fox Piven and Richard A. Cloward, "The Case Against Urban Desegregation," *Social Work* 12:12–21 (January 1967).

15. This same point is argued more completely by Charles V. Hamilton in "An Advocate of Black Power Defines It," *The New York Times Magazine*, April 14, 1968.

16. An earlier description of similar roles in social work is provided by Charles F. Grosser, "Community Development Programs Serving the Urban Poor," *Social Work* 10:15–21 (July 1965); also Richard A. Cloward and Frances F. Piven, "Birth of a Movement," *The Nation*, May 8, 1967; and Scott Briar, "The Casework Predicament," *Social Work* 13:5–11 (January 1968).

17. For a further discussion of this central point, see Irving L. Horowitz and Martin Liebowitz, "Social Deviance and Political Marginality: Toward a Redefinition of the Relation Between Sociology and Politics," *Social Problems* 15:280–296 (Winter 1968).

18. See, e.g., Briar, *op. cit.*, and other articles in the same issue dedicated to the late Gordon Hamilton, national social work leader and educator. For a "frankly angry response" to these articles from two social workers who are tired of hearing casework faulted, see Shirley Cooper and Barbara Krantzler, "A Polemic in Response to a Tribute," *Social Work* 13:3–4, 117–119 (April 1968).

19. Robert E. Gould, "Dr. Strangeclass: or How I Stopped Worrying About the Theory and Began Treating the Blue Collar Worker," *American Journal of Orthopsychiatry* 37:78–86 (January 1967).

20. This point is more fully discussed in Gerald M. Shattuck and John M. Martin, "New Professional Work Roles and Their Integration with Social Agency Structure," *Social Work* 14:13–20 (July 1969).

index

156